M000239208

ENDORSEMENTS

"Whether you are being introduced to a new restaurant or returning to your favorite cuisine, few things are as delightful as a sampler plate prepared by a master chef to give a taste of various delicacies. Such is this book. Sinclair Ferguson, a wise teacher of Christian theology and history, has given us a chef's tour of the Lord's sweet mercies across the last two thousand years. This is no bland synopsis. Ferguson's clear summaries of each century are festooned with juicy morsels taken from classic Christian writings and savory biographical stories. This little book will be a blessing to earnest Christians and a boon to those who would provide future generations with deeper roots in our rich Christian heritage."

—Dr. Joel R. Beeke
President and professor of systematic theology and homiletics
Puritan Reformed Theological Seminary, Grand Rapids, Mich.

"As a general rule, I give this counsel to everyone who will receive it: Read anything and everything by Sinclair Ferguson! This book is no exception. *In the Year of Our Lord: Reflections on Twenty Centuries of Church History* walks us through our Christian family history, in twenty short, easy-to-read chapters, always ultimately emphasizing the great work of Christ in preserving His church. There are tremendous lessons to increase our discernment and aid our encouragement stored up in this little book. Read, savor, and be edified."

—Dr. J. Ligon Duncan III
Chancellor
Reformed Theological Seminary

"There is nothing better to encourage, humble, and challenge Christians living in the Global South than to read how the Lord Jesus has kept His promise to build His church in other parts of the world since the beginning of Christianity. Dr. Ferguson's book made me weep and rejoice.

This is history told from the perspective of faith in God's promise. As biblical Christianity grows and expands in the Global South, we need to learn from the history of the church how God preserved His people in the midst of great suffering, and especially how He has preserved the true gospel through the ages in spite of so many errors that have threatened the church. As we face the grave errors of the neo-Pentecostal movement in Latin America, this book gives us hope in the God who has preserved His church always and everywhere."

—Dr. Augustus Nicodemus Lopes
Pastor
First Presbyterian Church, Goiânia, Brazil

"Church history as it should always be written—theologically grounded and pastorally applied. A marvelous read."

—Dr. Derek W.H. Thomas
Senior minister
First Presbyterian Church, Columbia, S.C.

In the Year of Our Lord

IN THE

YEAR

OF OUR

LORD

Reflections on
Twenty Centuries
of Church History

SINCLAIR B. FERGUSON

ℝ *Reformation Trust* A DIVISION OF LIGONIER MINISTRIES, ORLANDO, FL

In the Year of Our Lord: Reflections on Twenty Centuries of Church History
© 2018 by Sinclair B. Ferguson

Published by Reformation Trust Publishing
a division of Ligonier Ministries
421 Ligonier Court, Sanford, FL 32771
Ligonier.org   ReformationTrust.com

Printed in York, Pennsylvania
Maple Press
0000219
First edition, second printing

ISBN 978-1-56769-970-8 (Hardcover)
ISBN 978-1-56769-971-5 (ePub)
ISBN 978-1-56769-972-2 (Kindle)

All rights reserved. No part of this publication may be reproduced, stored in a retrieval system, or transmitted in any form or by any means—electronic, mechanical, photocopy, recording, or otherwise—without the prior written permission of the publisher, Reformation Trust Publishing. The only exception is brief quotations in printed reviews.

Cover design: Vanessa Wingo
Interior design and typeset: Katherine Lloyd, The DESK

Scripture quotations are from the ESV® Bible (The Holy Bible, English Standard Version®), copyright © 2001 by Crossway, a publishing ministry of Good News Publishers. Used by permission. All rights reserved.

Library of Congress Cataloging-in-Publication Data

Names: Ferguson, Sinclair B., author.
Title: In the year of our Lord : reflections on twenty centuries of church history / Sinclair B. Ferguson.
Description: Orlando, FL : Reformation Trust Publishing, 2018. | Includes bibliographical references and index.
Identifiers: LCCN 2018000985 (print) | LCCN 2018010877 (ebook) | ISBN 9781567699715 (E-book) | ISBN 9781567699722 (Mobi) | ISBN 9781567699708
Subjects: LCSH: Church history.
Classification: LCC BR145.3 (ebook) | LCC BR145.3 .F4765 2018 (print) | DDC 270--dc23
LC record available at https://lccn.loc.gov/2018000985

To
Vesta Sproul
and
in deep gratitude
for R.C.

CONTENTS

INTRODUCTION

The letters *AD* form the abbreviation for the Latin phrase *anno Domini*, which means "in the year of our Lord." It goes hand in hand with another abbreviation, BC, "before Christ."

At first glance, these seem to be a strange combination of languages. Why does AD indicate two words in Latin, whereas BC represents two English words? Perhaps the simplest answer is the correct one: the abbreviation for "before Christ" in Latin might also be AD (*ante Dominum*, "before our Lord").

Whatever the reason, a significant change has recently taken place in this time-honored tradition of dating. Now—especially in scholarly works—the letters CE (common era) and BCE (before the common era) have gradually replaced the traditional style.

This book retains the old style. It does so out of theological conviction, not simply out of antiquarian interests or from personal preference or, for that matter, out of prejudice. This change in format of dating history recognizes that we cannot avoid the significant impact on history of Jesus of Nazareth, but it removes from view His titles (Lord, Christ) and thus downplays both His personal uniqueness and His role in shaping our world-and-life view. In this sense, it is all of a piece with the radical transformations in worldviews that have taken place in the Western world over the past 250 years. The impact of what is usually referred to as the Enlightenment has gradually worn away the distinctiveness of the Christian faith in general and the incarnation as the center point of all history in particular.

The Change

Evidences for this change abound in the world of higher learning. The biblical mottoes of ancient universities are now abbreviated to disguise their origin. What were once known as faculties of theology or divinity have been renamed departments of religion or religious studies. In many places, what in the early European universities were the highest of the faculties have now been merged into the faculties of arts or social studies. In essence, they have become branches within the broader concept of anthropology (the study of man, his environment, and his philosophy and literature). The object of study is no longer God Himself (*theo*logy), but man and his spiritual experience (religion). The uniqueness of the Christian faith with its conviction that God became incarnate in Jesus Christ is now subordinated to what is common to all religious experience.

Against this background, the title *In the Year of Our Lord* has been deliberately chosen. For almost two thousand years now, the gospel of Jesus Christ has been preached and exemplified by men and women from virtually every corner of the globe. During that period, it has been the single most dominant influence on world history. Christ has left His mark indelibly on our world. These pages tell some of the stories of the two Christian millennia.

In the Year of Our Lord is not a history of the church. For one thing, its author is poorly qualified to attempt that, even in popular form. Rather, *In the Year of Our Lord* is more like a personal tour of some of the people and places its author has encountered over the years.

But why turn that into a book?

Hegel's Lament

In one sense, it is because we can never know enough about our Christian family. But we modern people tend to be so enamored of the present, so engulfed by contemporary media, that we know very little about history before our own lifetime. As the philosopher Hegel once lamented, we learn from history that we learn nothing from history. Taken at face value, this judgment sounds both harsh and cynical. It is, however, not without evidence.

In the closing weeks of 1999, in the run-up to what was commonly thought of as the close of the second millennium and the opening of the third, one of the best-selling popular newspapers in the United Kingdom published the results of a poll it had sponsored. The findings underlined my suspicions about our general knowledge of history. Readers were asked to name the most significant man and the most significant woman of the previous millennium, AD 1000–2000.

The winners?

Male: Nelson Mandela.

Female: Princess Diana.

Doubtless, reactions to these names differ widely. Perhaps, indeed, they were the two most "celebrated" or iconic figures of the second half of the twentieth century. But what of the 950 preceding years? And what did this result reveal about the average reader? Probably that we know almost nothing about history beyond what we have been fed by the popular media.

It would be easy to be cynical and to go beyond even Hegel's lament by saying that now we learn no history!

If this is true in general in our society, then it is also likely to be true of Christians. But Christians, by definition, have an interest in history, for a particular view of history and its importance is built into the Christian faith. The faith is founded in the long story narrated in the Old Testament, and its focus is on Jesus Christ as its climax. We may not be professional historians (although some Christians are). We may not know all of the facts of history (who does?). But we understand the deep significance of the past for the present. We believe that history has a pattern and a goal. And, in addition, we belong to the Christian family, which not only stretches throughout the world, but also back into history. So, history is important to us.

Yet, despite this, it is perhaps also true that we Christians do not know as much as we feel we should.

The poverty of our knowledge of the past is by no means entirely our own fault. In recent years, our Christian subculture has paid little heed to the past, in terms of the literature we have read (usually "the latest thing"), the songs we have sung (frequently contemporary, non-Trinitarian, rarely

3

expressing lament, often oriented toward the self), and the worship in which we have engaged (often pleasure-seeking rather than God-centered, graded occasionally by organizations expert in the field rather than by God and His Word).

If this is so, then we have denied ourselves some of the greatest delights of walking the Christian way. For we possess a vast multitude of brothers and sisters in Christ from whose lives we can learn, through whose stories we can be challenged and encouraged, by whose writings we can be instructed, and by whose hymns we can be inspired to worship and live with greater devotion to our Lord.

Tracing the Story

Against this background, *In the Year of Our Lord* is intended to be a very simple but (I hope) informative, encouraging, and enjoyable introduction to some members of "the Christian family"—the worldwide, history-deep, eternity-long church of Jesus Christ. It is a book of people, stories, words, and songs—a kind of family narrative accompanied by a songbook. It is not a history of the church, but simply fragments of her story. It is not the work of a professional historian but of a family member. It does not tell the whole story, only that part that specially belongs to the Christians with whom the author has most rubbed shoulders.

Thus, *In the Year of Our Lord* traces parts of a grand narrative that flows from first-century Jerusalem to the present day. But that narrative divides into many smaller narratives along the way to the twenty-first century. Were the story written by an African or Chinese or Latin American or Lebanese or Russian or Korean Christian, the story of how the gospel got to his or her "here" from within the same grand narrative would inevitably follow different twists and turns along the way. In some instances, the road would divide earlier; in others, later. To tell the whole story, even in brief form, would require a large volume indeed. Indeed, we might apply the words of the (presumably smiling) Apostle John that if we were to recount all the great works of Christ by the Spirit in the past two thousand years, the whole world would not be able to contain the books that would need to be written (John 21:25).

Nobody Is Perfect

In the world of twentieth-century moral philosophy, a view known formally as "emotivism" was held by a number of thinkers. Its basic tenet was that moral judgments are not objective statements of fact but simply expressions of approval or disapproval, likes or dislikes. According to this theory, when I say something is "good," I mean little more than "I like it." By the same token, if I say it is "bad," I am simply saying, "I don't like it." Emotivism is an ethical philosophy without moral absolutes, and ultimately therefore without real moral power. It has been well caricatured as "The Boo-Hurrah Theory of Ethics" ("bad"="boo"—I don't like it; "good"="hurrah"—I do like it).

It is possible to fall into a similar "boo-hurrah" approach when we survey the story of the church, mistakenly pigeonholing individuals or movements as either wholly saintly or wholly reprehensible. Thus, evangelical Christians will find it easy to say "hurrah!" for the names of Athanasius, Augustine, and Luther, but "boo!" for Arius, Pelagius, and Socinus—and so on. And sometimes we do so without any firsthand knowledge of what they wrote and taught.

But even our heroes have feet of clay, and it is important to try to see professing Christians in the context in which they actually lived. Christian faith knows only one perfect man and one perfect work— Jesus Christ. Every saint, every work, every movement is a mixture of God's gracious operations and our often sinful and inadequate actions. So, none of the figures featured in these pages was perfect. Some of them did much good, wrote much that is helpful, and demonstrated enormous courage. But sometimes they also did harm by their inadequate or confused teaching about the Christian faith or by the style in which they lived it. Like us, both personally and intellectually, their sanctification was not complete. So what we can honor and imitate we should, but we ought never to be blinded by unthinking admiration.

At the end of the day, the source, the praise, for all that is good belongs to the Lord. Yet at the same time, He wants us to be thankful for the gifts He has given to men and women to help us on the way. We are called to learn from them, to admire their labors in the gospel, and to imitate them insofar as they imitated Christ (see 1 Cor. 4:16; 11:1; Phil. 3:17; 1 Thess. 1:6; 2 Thess. 3:7, 9; Heb. 13:7). It would be myopic, therefore, if we expected that a book like this, however brief and superficial, would describe only the perfect.

Almost every student of the Apostolic Fathers (the men who immediately followed the Apostolic period) is struck by the huge difference between the clarity and power of the Apostles' teaching and the sometimes impoverished grasp of the gospel in the writings that followed only decades later. John ("Rabbi") Duncan, professor of Hebrew at the Free Church College in Edinburgh, Scotland, expressed a wise perspective when he spoke of Polycarp, the second-century bishop (minister) of the church in Smyrna, who in his eighties was martyred for his confession of faith in Christ: "Polycarp would have stood a bad chance in an examination by John Owen"[1]; elsewhere he notes, "But oh, Polycarp and these men were notable men, to burn for the cause of Christ."[2]

Duncan understood what we will see again and again in these pages: that it is possible to have hearts that have been washed cleaner than our heads. Sometimes it will be hard for us to appreciate why Christians did not better understand the gospel. But then, we are often unaware of the privileges we have enjoyed because of the context in which we have lived our Christian lives—where each of us has our own copy (probably multiple copies) of the Scriptures and access to Christian literature and a wide array of helpful biblical teachers. Thankfully, our Lord providentially overrules our weaknesses without minimizing our responsibility for our mistakes. He has never gone back on His promise: "I will build my church, and the gates of hell shall not prevail against it" (Matt. 16:18).

The Church-Building Program

Jesus is always building His church. He has been creating His new covenant community for two thousand years. And He has been doing so in enemy-occupied territory. The gates of Hades may withstand, but can never prevent, His ultimate triumph.

Christ's kingdom is advancing. It has not done so, as far as we can see, in a straight line, like a steadily and consistently rising graph. Indeed, in keeping with the biblical plotline, it appears to advance in epochs and on occasion seems hidden and almost dormant. At times and in certain places, it seems to suffer great loss, and at other times and places it makes great gains.

Thus, today, in many parts of the West, the professing church is marked by rapid numerical decline and suffers from a hardening of the spiritual heart arteries. Meanwhile, elsewhere the church experiences persecution and great suffering, and yet through this it grows and makes great advances. It is not insignificant that the twentieth century may have witnessed more martyrs for Christ than any century since the beginning of the church. Yet at the same time, more people have become professing Christians than ever before.

The river of the church's story flows into the whole of our modern world, north and south, east and west. One book could not possibly tell the whole story.

There is an important difference between a panorama and a vista, although the two words seem frequently to be confused or treated as synonyms. This little book is intended to be both: a panorama in the sense that it covers twenty centuries of the life of the Christian church, but a vista—a narrow view—in the sense that it is written by a Scottish Presbyterian whose church experience has been largely confined to the United Kingdom and the United States. I hope it will inform, challenge, and stimulate to further exploration. Remembering Hegel's lament, I have interspersed the story of the past with some lessons we might take to heart for the life of the present and future church.

I hope these fragments of the church's story will encourage the assurance that the Lord Jesus has indeed been building His church and will continue to do so until He comes again in majesty and glory.

The format of each chapter is simple: it opens with a quotation on which to reflect, followed by a brief narrative of individuals and events from that century. Each chapter concludes with a hymn written in the same century. I hope these pages will express something of the flavor of the Christian life, tell the story of the advance of the gospel, and give some sense of the worship of the church throughout the ages.

Origins

In centuries past, it was customary for authors to express their reluctance to rush into print by saying in a preface that their book was being published because of the desire of friends that material they had heard or privately read might reach a wider audience. These pages fall into that category. Their origin lies in a series of talks I gave in our church during the closing months of 1999 when the turn of the millennium was uppermost in many people's thinking. Having long held the suspicion that many Christians know very little about the great family history of the church, I decided to take a few minutes early on in our evening worship to talk about each of the Christian centuries. That segment of our worship (which in some ways I justified on the basis that the Apostolic letters themselves do precisely this—provide Christians with information about fellow believers elsewhere) was always climaxed with the singing of a hymn written in the century about which I had been speaking.

It is one thing for someone with some knowledge of church history and the story of theology to sit down for a few minutes and think of interesting and informative people and events in the passing of a century and to give a brief talk; it is quite another to accede to requests to put the material into writing. What can be hidden in a talk is exposed when put down on paper with no personal context! But now, stimulated by various considerations, the opportunity has arisen to expand that simple material into book length.[3] *In the Year of Our Lord* represents a much fuller and, I hope, richer form of this material. I am grateful to Reformation Trust and the staff of Ligonier Ministries who in this, as in so many other things, have given me every encouragement. As always, my wife, Dorothy, has provided the mainstay of human love that has made it possible for me to devote time and energy to writing.

A Man with a Dream

Authors sometimes dream that their books will accomplish more than one goal. Books can, it is hoped, be enjoyed by their readers. But a book can also be the means by which an author can express his or her affection and appreciation for others by way of the time-honored tradition of a dedication. *In the Year of Our Lord* has been written with both of these goals in view.

Many years ago, over dinner, a young man told me of a vivid dream he had experienced. In it, he had seen an army of theologians coming over the brow of a hill and marching toward him out of the past. How he knew they were theologians was, I think, part of the mystery of the dreamworld. He could make out Augustine, Martin Luther, John Calvin, Jonathan Edwards, and other great figures from the past. But the striking feature of the dream was that they were all being led toward him by someone he also recognized—a contemporary Christian leader who, through his ministry of teaching, preaching, and writing, had first introduced these heroes of the faith to my young host. That someone was R.C. Sproul.

In all likelihood, no one in the late twentieth and early twenty-first centuries has introduced as many ordinary Christians to the story and theology of the church as did R.C. In that task he was constantly encouraged by his wife, Vesta. Through four decades, R.C. and Vesta befriended and encouraged me. In addition, they gave me many privileged opportunities to share in the remarkable and multifaceted work of Ligonier Ministries, which began life in Western Pennsylvania and now touches the far corners of the earth.

R.C. went to be with his Lord on December 14, 2017. He was a good soldier in Christ's army and a faithful servant of God, with an outstanding intellect and great gifts. But he was also my friend, and it was in large measure out of a desire to thank him and Vesta that this book was first written. It is with deep gratitude for their friendship and fellowship in the ministry of the gospel that this book is dedicated to them.

1

THE FIRST CENTURY

THE EARLY GROWTH
OF THE CHURCH

*John the Divine sees the whole story of the church in a vivid vision
full of biblical allusions. The following text is from Revelation 12.*

And a great sign appeared in heaven: a woman clothed with the
sun, with the moon under her feet, and on her head a crown of
twelve stars. She was pregnant and was crying out in birth pains and
the agony of giving birth. And another sign appeared in heaven:
behold, a great red dragon, with seven heads and ten horns, and on
his heads seven diadems. His tail swept down a third of the stars of
heaven and cast them to the earth. And the dragon stood before the
woman who was about to give birth, so that when she bore her child
he might devour it. She gave birth to a male child, one who is to
rule all the nations with a rod of iron, but her child was caught up
to God and to his throne, and the woman fled into the wilderness,
where she has a place prepared by God, in which she is to be nourished for 1,260 days.

Now war arose in heaven, Michael and his angels fighting against
the dragon. And the dragon and his angels fought back, but he was

defeated, and there was no longer any place for them in heaven. And the great dragon was thrown down, that ancient serpent, who is called the devil and Satan, the deceiver of the whole world—he was thrown down to the earth, and his angels were thrown down with him. And I heard a loud voice in heaven, saying, "Now the salvation and the power and the kingdom of our God and the authority of his Christ have come, for the accuser of our brothers has been thrown down, who accuses them day and night before our God. And they have conquered him by the blood of the Lamb and by the word of their testimony, for they loved not their lives even unto death. Therefore, rejoice, O heavens and you who dwell in them! But woe to you, O earth and sea, for the devil has come down to you in great wrath, because he knows that his time is short!"

And when the dragon saw that he had been thrown down to the earth, he pursued the woman who had given birth to the male child. But the woman was given the two wings of the great eagle so that she might fly from the serpent into the wilderness, to the place where she is to be nourished for a time, and times, and half a time. The serpent poured water like a river out of his mouth after the woman, to sweep her away with a flood. But the earth came to the help of the woman, and the earth opened its mouth and swallowed the river that the dragon had poured from his mouth. Then the dragon became furious with the woman and went off to make war on the rest of her offspring, on those who keep the commandments of God and hold to the testimony of Jesus. And he stood on the sand of the sea.

———

What do you know about the first century of the Christian church? It divides into three periods. The first third of it should be most familiar to every Christian. Somewhere around the year AD 30, Simon called Peter, a fisherman from Galilee, confessed that Jesus of Nazareth was the long-expected Jewish Messiah and the Son of God. Jesus in turn promised His small group of disciples, "I will build my church, and the gates of hell shall not prevail against it" (Matt. 16:18).

This is a key statement in world history. Twenty centuries later, we can see that Jesus' promise has proved breathtakingly true.

We must not run ahead of the story. Yet simply to read these words is to sense that they have a programmatic ring to them.

Why He Came

"Christ Jesus came into the world to save sinners," Paul wrote (1 Tim. 1:15), echoing the confession of the early church, according to which the essence of the Christian gospel is this:

> Christ died for our sins in accordance with the Scriptures, that he was buried, that he was raised on the third day in accordance with the Scriptures, and that he appeared to Cephas, then to the twelve. (1 Cor. 15:1–3)

But He did this not merely to save isolated individuals. If one of the disciples had asked Jesus, "What did You come into the world to achieve?" He would have said, "To seek and to save the lost." But He would also have emphasized, "I also came into the world to build a church, a new community of redeemed people." And so He lived and taught, did works of mighty power, died on the cross, and rose again from the dead in order to fulfill this promise—"I will build my church."

The Apostle John provides a further perspective on the ministry of his Savior: "The reason the Son of God appeared was to destroy the works of the devil" (1 John 3:8). In one sense, these words encompass the entire plotline of the Bible from the beginning to the end. Immediately after the fall, God pronounced a judgment curse on the tempter.

There would be ongoing enmity between his offspring and the offspring of Eve:

> I will put enmity between you and the woman,
>   and between your offspring and her offspring;
> he shall bruise your head,
>   and you shall bruise his heel. (Gen. 3:15)

The Longest Footnote?

The philosopher Alfred North Whitehead once wrote that "the safest general characterization of the European philosophical tradition is that it consists in a series of footnotes to Plato."[1] In the same way, we might say the story of the Old Testament is a series of footnotes to Genesis 3:15. Every stage in the Old Testament's development toward the coming of Christ is marked by conflict, sometimes personal, sometimes national, occasionally both. When Jesus stepped onto the stage of history, that conflict came to a crisis point. The *Serpent himself* now faced *the* Seed of the woman. This is why Luke (who clearly had a special interest in redemptive history) traces Jesus' genealogy back to Adam (and not only to Abraham, as Matthew does; Luke 3:23–38; see Matt. 1:1–17).

The Gospels tell the story of three years of conflict between the Lord Jesus and the powers of darkness, beginning with His installation into His public role as Messiah and His victory over Satan in the wilderness.[2]

Thereafter, Jesus' ministry is marked by His doing the following:

1. Engaging in ongoing conflict with the opposition mounted against Him by "the seed of the serpent" ("You are of your father the devil," Jesus told some of His opponents [John 8:44])
2. Expressing His victory by the way He set free those who were bound by sin, sickness, or demonic possession
3. Teaching His disciples about the power and lifestyle of the kingdom
4. Facing the final conflict with Satan in Gethsemane and Calvary, rising victoriously from the grave, and ascending to be enthroned over all powers

Christ died for our sins. But in addition, through His obedience and sacrifice, He defeated the Evil One and regained the dominion that Adam forfeited. That is why "all authority in heaven *and on earth*" now belongs to Jesus and is to be realized through the church's mission of taking the gospel to the ends of the earth (Matt. 28:18–20, emphasis added).

This leads into the second period of the first century. Its key text is again found in words of Jesus, this time spoken between His resurrection and His ascension. He told His disciples that they would be His witnesses, first in Jerusalem, then in Judea, then in Samaria, and ultimately to the farthest parts of the earth (Acts 1:8).

Early Growth

The Acts of the Apostles records the events of the second period, the next twenty to thirty years of the first century, and illustrates how the promise of Jesus was fulfilled. In essence, it chronicles the continuing acts of the ascended Christ effected by the Spirit in the lives of the Apostles and the first Christians. Jesus poured out His Holy Spirit upon the Apostles and others who gathered in Jerusalem on the day of Pentecost. In the second chapter of Acts, Luke carefully records how people from different parts of the ancient world heard the first Christian sermon and responded in repentance and faith to its gospel message. Many of them must have returned home almost immediately and spread the gospel throughout the ancient world, telling others about the great things Jesus had done. A later wave of mission-by-scattering is recorded in Acts 8 when many of the disciples were forced to flee Jerusalem because of the persecution that followed the martyrdom of Stephen.

Thus, within two months of Jesus' death, the story of His life, death, resurrection, ascension, and giving of the Spirit was already being spread throughout the Roman Empire. The rest of the Acts of the Apostles (really the ongoing acts of Jesus by His Spirit through the Apostles) tells the story of the multiplication of the church. It concludes with Paul, once the arch-persecutor of Jesus, now in Rome, the epicenter of secular power, "proclaiming the kingdom of God and teaching about the Lord Jesus Christ with all boldness and without hindrance" (Acts 28:31).

In between Acts 2 and Acts 28, Luke's narrative is full of punctuation marks. He regularly presses the pause button in order to give a progress report on all that God is doing (see, for example, 2:41, 47; 5:14; 6:1, 7; 9:31; 12:24; 16:5; 19:20).

Acts also tells us how the gospel broke out into the Gentile world through the preaching of Simon Peter (10:1–11:18). Since that time, it has not stopped going to the ends of the earth.

Apostolic Travels

The rest of the New Testament gives us hints of how widely the Apostles traveled—although, with the exception of Paul, they were all born in the same very small country—in order to make the message of the gospel known.

Peter's ministry opened the door to the kingdom on the day of Pentecost. Later, he would be instrumental in the gospel's being preached to the Gentiles. But his main ministry seems to have been to Jewish believers (see Gal. 2:7). We know from his letters that he had contact with the churches in what we now call Turkey (1 Peter 1:1).

Paul's ministry was exercised in various Roman provinces throughout modern-day Turkey and into Europe. The Acts of the Apostles, which begins with Jesus' promise that the Apostles would go far and wide to preach the gospel, ends with Paul, formerly the great persecutor of the church but now become Apostle to the Gentiles, preaching in Rome. Indeed, the last verse of Acts forms a significant bookend to the entire narrative that began with Acts 1:8: in Rome, Paul "welcomed all who came to him, proclaiming the kingdom of God and teaching about the Lord Jesus Christ with all boldness *and without hindrance*" (28:30–31, emphasis added).

The New Testament tells us relatively little about the third part of the story of the church's expansion or the history of the other Apostles.

John, we know, was exiled on the island of Patmos, where he experienced the vision recorded in the book of Revelation.[3] The traditions of the church suggest that some of the other Apostles traveled great distances to preach Christ.

Thomas seems to have preached in Persia. According to church tradition, he preached the gospel in India also. (It is claimed he was martyred near Madras.) Still today, the Mar-Thoma Church (the church of St. Thomas) traces its origins back to his preaching in the modern Indian state of Kerala. While it is often impossible to penetrate behind these traditions, they nevertheless are a testimony to the remarkable spread of the gospel and the transforming power of the Spirit. These men who once deserted Christ devoted their lives to preaching Him to the ends of the earth.

The Apostles themselves tasted the firstfruits of the harsh persecutions that became a keynote of the closing decades of the first century and the days that followed. Right from its inauguration, the church of Jesus Christ has been built on territory formerly under the sway of the Evil One (1 John 5:19). Not surprisingly, wherever the gospel advanced, it faced opposition, intimidation, and suffering.

Persecution under Nero

Already in the 60s, the emperor Nero had turned upon Christians. Rome had burned. Rumor had it that the conflagration was started by Nero himself. In order to fend off accusations against himself, the emperor blamed the Christians. A "circus of blood" followed. Believers were crucified like their Master. Some were sewn within the skins of dead animals and thrown to wild dogs to be torn to pieces. On one occasion, Nero had Christians covered in pitch, raised up on poles all around Rome, and set ablaze in order to light the city with dying believers.

Reflecting on these days, Tertullian, the second-century Latin author, wrote in his *Apology*[4] for the Christian faith that the gospel was triumphing not only despite the opposition but, in the purposes of God, partly because of it. He wrote to the Roman emperor, "We are but of yesterday, yet we fill your cities, islands, forts, towns, councils, even camps, tribes, decuries, the palace, the senate, the forum; we have left you the temples alone."[5] As he looked back on the previous decades, he wrote, "The blood of Christians is seed."[6]

Thus, the gospel spread, and as Jesus promised, the church was being built, notwithstanding the opposition of the gates of Hades. From the vantage point of our own century, we can rejoice as we look back on the faithfulness of our Lord throughout those critical early days of the first-century church. He kept His promise then; He is still keeping it today. He will never stop building His church, and He will always be with His people until He returns to glorify them. Then He will be with them forever.

At the Name of Jesus—
the Christ Hymn of Philippians 2:5–11 (c. AD 60)

CAROLINE NOEL (1870)

At the Name of Jesus, every knee shall bow,
Every tongue confess Him King of glory now;
'Tis the Father's pleasure we should call Him Lord,
Who from the beginning was the mighty Word.

Mighty and mysterious in the highest height,
God from everlasting, very light of light:
In the Father's bosom with the spirit blest,
Love, in love eternal, rest, in perfect rest.

At His voice creation sprang at once to sight,
All the angel faces, all the hosts of light,
Thrones and dominations, stars upon their way,
All the heavenly orders, in their great array.

Humbled for a season, to receive a name
From the lips of sinners unto whom He came,
Faithfully He bore it, spotless to the last,
Brought it back victorious when from death He passed.

Bore it up triumphant with its human light,
Through all ranks of creatures, to the central height,
To the throne of Godhead, to the Father's breast;
Filled it with the glory of that perfect rest.

Name Him, brothers, name Him, with love strong as death
But with awe and wonder, and with bated breath!
He is God the Saviour, He is Christ the Lord,
Ever to be worshipped, trusted and adored.

In your hearts enthrone Him; there let Him subdue
All that is not holy, all that is not true;

Crown Him as your Captain in temptation's hour;
Let His will enfold you in its light and power.

Brothers, this Lord Jesus shall return again,
With His Father's glory, with His angel train;
For all wreaths of empire meet upon His brow,
And our hearts confess Him King of glory now.

2

THE SECOND CENTURY

TROUBLES INSIDE
AND OUTSIDE

Though he was by no means the only martyr in the second century, Poly-carp's story is particularly moving since he was born at the end of the Apostolic era and may well have been a Christian believer longer than anyone else in the world when he was martyred. The following text is excerpted from The Martyrdom of Polycarp.

But without being disturbed, and as if suffering nothing, he went eagerly forward with all haste, and was conducted to the stadium, where the tumult was so great, that there was no possibility of being heard. Now, as Polycarp was entering into the stadium, there came to him a voice from heaven, saying, "Be strong, and show yourself a man, O Polycarp!" No one saw who it was that spoke to him; but those of our brethren who were present heard the voice. And as he was brought forward, the tumult became great when they heard that Polycarp was taken. And when he came near, the proconsul asked him whether he was Polycarp. On his confessing that he was, [the proconsul] sought to persuade him to deny [Christ], saying, "Have respect to your old age," and other similar things, according to their custom, [such as], "Swear by the fortune of Caesar; repent, and say, 'Away with the Atheists.'" But Polycarp, gazing with a stern countenance on all the multitude of the wicked heathen then in the stadium, and waving his hand towards them, while with groans he looked up to heaven, said, "Away with the Atheists." Then, the proconsul urging him, and saying, "Swear, and I will set you at liberty, reproach Christ"; Polycarp declared, "Eighty and six years have I served Him, and He never did me any injury: how then can I blaspheme my King and my Saviour?"

And when the proconsul yet again pressed him, and said, "Swear by the fortune of Caesar," he answered, "Since you are vainly urgent that, as you say, I should swear by the fortune of Caesar, and pretend not to know who and what I am, hear me declare with boldness, I am a Christian. And if you wish to learn what the doctrines of Christianity are, appoint me a day, and you shall hear them." The proconsul replied, "Persuade the people." But Polycarp said, "To you I have thought it right to offer an account [of my faith]; for we are taught to give all due honour (which entails no injury upon ourselves) to the powers and authorities which are ordained of God. But as for *these*, I do not deem them worthy of receiving any account from me."

The proconsul then said to him, "I have wild beasts at hand; to these will I cast you, unless you repent." But he answered, "Call them then, for we are not accustomed to repent of what is good in order to adopt that which is evil; and it is well for me to be changed from what is evil to what is righteous." But again the proconsul said to him, "I will cause you to be consumed by fire, seeing you despise the wild beasts, if you will not repent." But Polycarp said, "You threaten me with fire which burns for an hour, and after a little is extinguished, but are ignorant of the fire of the coming judgment and of eternal punishment, reserved for the ungodly. But why do you tarry? Bring forth what you will." . . .

This, then, was carried into effect with greater speed than it was spoken. . . .

———

Matthew 16:18, as we have seen, is a pivotal text in the New Testament. It tells us not only that Jesus will build His church, but that He will do so in enemy-occupied territory.

Satan does not yield ground easily, however. Wherever Christ builds, opposition will develop. As we read about the Christian centuries and live in the contemporary world, we need to learn this: gospel advance always evokes opposition. That is as true in our personal lives as it is in the life of the church.

In the second century, opposition to the Christian faith came in two different forms.

Persecution

The first form of opposition was *blatant persecution*. The revelation given to John on Patmos provided the church with striking insight into what to expect. John saw a great red dragon (identified as the serpent of Eden grown large) seeking to destroy Christ. Failing to do so, he then sets off in pursuit of the offspring of the woman. The opposition of the serpent and his seed to the seed of the woman continues, but the holy seed is preserved by the power of God (Rev. 12).

Jesus Christ, the Savior of sinners, is always first seen by sinners as a threat. This is why we hide from Him or oppose Him, resisting the witness of His disciples and in various ways defending ourselves and opposing them. It should not surprise us, therefore, that a major subtheme of church history is the ongoing opposition of those whose aim is the destruction of the church. Behind this opposition lies a supernatural, spiritual strategy permanently set against the building program of the Lord Jesus (2 Cor. 10:3–4; Eph. 6:12).

Paradoxically, however, as Tertullian wrote, "The blood of Christians is seed." Jesus Christ has built His church through the centuries by permitting suffering and martyrdom. Did He not say, "Unless a grain of wheat falls into the earth and dies, it remains alone; but if it dies, it bears much fruit" (John 12:24)?

Sheltered

In its infancy, the church was given shelter because of its Jewish roots. Judaism was a *religio licita*—a "permitted religion"—in the Roman Empire. Jews were not officially persecuted under government policy. Indeed, some were Roman citizens (Saul of Tarsus, for one). We know there were Romans who were sympathetic to the Jewish faith (including the centurion who built the Capernaum synagogue and Cornelius, who invited Peter to come to his house to preach the gospel; see Luke 7:1–10; Acts 10:1ff.). Even in "Caesar's household" Christians could be found (see Phil. 4:22).

But by the beginning of the second century, it had become clear that a great gulf existed between Jews and Christians. Although they claimed the same origins, these were two different kinds of people. Both the Bible and the ancient world spoke about two races of men—either Jews and gentiles, or Greeks and barbarians. But by the end of the second century Tertullian could speak of a "third race of men." There were still Jews and gentiles, but Christians were regarded as neither;[1] they constituted a new humanity.

Christos Kurios or *Kaesar Kurios*?

Christians spoke of a historical figure—Jesus of Nazareth—as *Kurios*, "Lord." They did not, and would not, confess Caesar as Lord—the self-styled claim of the emperor Domitian,[2] who called himself "Lord and God." To refuse to make that confession was not merely a matter of private religious conviction; it was a form of rebellion against the empire—treason, a capital offense. And so, many Christians, especially those regarded as leaders in the churches, were martyred for their resolute faith. Domitian is infamous for charging his cousin Flavius Clemens, himself a Roman consul, with atheism[3] and for banishing Clemens' wife, Domitilla—very possibly because they had become Christians.[4]

A season of relative calm followed Domitian's reign, although on occasion Christian women were tortured on the rack. In the second decade of the century, Ignatius, the bishop (or minister) of the church in Antioch, was condemned, taken to Rome, and devoured by lions in the Colosseum.[5]

Some forty years later, Ignatius was followed to a martyr's death by Polycarp.[6] Arrested and brought before the Roman authorities at the end of the public games held in the Smyrna stadium, Polycarp was urged to acknowledge that Caesar was Lord. This remarkable and endearing old man refused to do so, and famously confessed, "I have served Jesus Christ these eighty and six years. He has done me no harm; why should I deny him now?" He was summarily executed. Others, including young people, were put to death for the sake of their simple testimony to Jesus Christ.

Yesterday Returns Today

It is particularly significant for us today to realize what these early Christians were doing. They were not being asked to say that Caesar is the *only lord*, only that *Jesus is not the only Lord*. Roman religion was polytheistic. It recognized all kinds of gods, including Caesar.[7] It was therefore not a problem for the state if a person believed in a wide variety of gods, each appropriate to his personal activities—so long as he also swore loyalty to the emperor and the empire by saying "Caesar is Lord." Even to say "Yahweh is Lord" could be tolerated (was He not, after all, simply another local god—the God of the Jews?).

But Jesus was different. He had appeared on the scene of history and had "suffered under Pontius Pilate"—a Roman governor. He was not a remote God but a historical figure—as real, and recent, as Claudius Caesar himself. It was clear that His lordship could not be confessed alongside that of other lords, for when Christians said, "Jesus is Lord," they clearly meant that He alone and no other is Lord. Therein lay the grounds for faithful Christians to be accused of, and tried for, the capital offense of treason.

Merely History?

We are not in such a stage in the Western world, although elsewhere the church is under that threat. Yet it is becoming increasingly clear in our society that while the lordship of Jesus Christ may be permitted as a private religious conviction, for an individual to act in a manner consistent with that conviction may well contravene laws created by the state. Confessing Jesus as Lord is permitted, but to express His lordship may be a different issue altogether.

In this respect, unless a major social transformation takes place, Christians are increasingly likely to find themselves living in societies that share the norms of the anti-Christian emperors. There is therefore much for us to learn from the God-given courage of these early Christians whose blood became the seed of the church.

Fatal Poison

But another kind of opposition to the building of the church was present in the second century: *false teaching*.

Whenever we interpret the gospel for a culture, there is always the danger of syncretism—adapting our message for the receiving culture and in the process diluting the message we convey. Thus, when people respond, they meld the gospel to their own previous convictions. The result is a mixture of gospel and paganism.

Syncretism is always a danger. It happens easily in the first communication of the gospel, and it can happen again and again even where the gospel has taken root. Thus, for example, the message of the cross transforms manners, for Christian love brings with it gentleness, grace, thoughtfulness, kindness, putting others first, and so on. But when the power of the cross is diluted, its fruit often remains for a season. But then this is confused with the thing itself—as though Christianity were identical to culture.

In the second century, Hellenistic philosophy crafted the lenses through which everything was viewed. In that sense, it was the influence that invisibly shaped how people thought. Of particular note, it regarded spirit as pure and good and matter as inherently evil.

When the gospel was seen through those lenses, it was not long before it was distorted in some fundamental ways. If spirit alone is good and matter is by definition evil, it is impossible that a good God could have created a material world. How then did the world come into being? It must have been created by a lower kind of deity—a god emanating

26

somehow from the Perfect One. This "creator god" was known as the *demiurge*—a less-than-perfect god. This, in turn, became the lens through which the revelation of God in the Old Testament was viewed.

The staying power of this misshapen theology has been remarkable. It still finds its way into the thinking of people who "prefer" the "New Testament God" to the "Old Testament God." They see the latter as angry and wrathful and the former as loving and kind. But this in turn means that the New Testament itself needs to be read in a very selective way, since the God who reveals Himself there *is* the God who revealed Himself in the Old Testament. Of course, what eventually happens is that we create a god in our own image—and add to the already heavily populated pantheon of the "how I like to think about God" gods.

A second repercussion of this perspective is the belief that *God could never become incarnate.* In this world-and-life view, spirit and flesh are antithetical. The incarnation must therefore be only apparent. The Son of God only *seemed* to take our human nature.[8] By contrast, the Gospels make clear that Christ was truly and fully human. He felt hunger, thirst, sorrow, and pain.

Clear-thinking theologians recognized the danger here: if Christ was only apparently human, He could not save those who are truly and fully human—and fallen. For if He is not really one of us, He cannot act as our substitute and representative.[9]

These twin errors of falsely equating the material with the sinful and setting the physical over against the spiritual continue to linger in the Christian church. They are illustrated in the way the idea of the immortality of the soul has taken the place of the New Testament's teaching of the regeneration of the cosmos and the resurrection of the flesh. Thus, both God's creation of man at the beginning of time and His re-creation of man at the end become distorted.

So, the Christian church was under attack on two fronts—physical persecution and false teaching. On the one hand was the threat of martyrdom, and on the other was the threat of heresy. One of these enemies is much more dangerous than the other—but it is not, as we might think, persecution. The early Christians knew that martyrdom could never ultimately kill either the believer or the church. But false teaching always does.

We modern Christians tend to assume it is the other way around. We have little fear of false teaching but considerable fear of persecution. And yet, of all generations, perhaps ours is the one that should have learned to think most clearly and biblically. Think of China in our own time and compare it to any country in Europe. The church in China has not been destroyed by suffering. Rather, the blood of martyrs has been seed. But in Europe? The church has been largely shielded from persecution. In the process, it has naively tolerated what has been well described as "the cruelty of heresy."[10] There has been much false teaching. The consequences are visible for all to see in the powerlessness of a church whose views have often become indistinguishable from those of the world.

If we find the thought of suffering for the gospel surprising, we may already have imbibed false teaching. At the very least, we have ignored biblical teaching: "Beloved, do not be surprised at the fiery trial when it comes upon you to test you, as though something strange were happening to you. But rejoice insofar as you share Christ's sufferings, that you may also rejoice and be glad when his glory is revealed" (1 Peter 4:12–13). Let those who have ears to hear listen.

Shepherd of Tender Youth, Guiding in Love and Truth

Clement of Alexandria (c. 155–220)

Shepherd of tender youth, guiding in love and truth
Through devious ways; Christ our triumphant king,
We come Thy name to sing and here our children bring
To join Thy praise.

Thou art our holy Lord, O all subduing Word,
Healer of strife. Thou didst Thyself abase
That from sin's deep disgrace Thou mightest save our race
And give us life.

Thou art the great high priest; Thou hast prepared the feast
Of holy love; and in our mortal pain,
None calls on Thee in vain; help Thou dost not disdain,
Help from above.

Ever be Thou our guide, our shepherd and our pride,
Our staff and song; Jesus, Thou Christ of God,
By Thine enduring Word lead us where Thou hast trod,
Make our faith strong.

So now, and till we die, sound we Thy praises high
And joyful sing; infants and the glad throng
Who to Thy church belong, unite to swell the song
To Christ, our king.

3

———

THE THIRD CENTURY

THE APOLOGISTS

Tertullian was not only a brave apologist for the Christian gospel but the theologian who provided some of the most basic Christian vocabulary used by the church in all future generations. The following text is excerpted from **The Apology of Tertullian.**

If we are enjoined, then, to love our enemies, as I have remarked above, whom have we to hate? If injured, we are forbidden to retaliate, lest we become as bad ourselves: who can suffer injury at our hands? In regard to this, recall your own experiences. How often you inflict gross cruelties on Christians, partly because it is your own inclination, and partly in obedience to the laws! How often, too, the hostile mob, paying no regard to you, takes the law into its own hand, and assails us with stones and flames! With the very frenzy of the Bacchanals, they do not even spare the Christian dead, but tear them, now sadly changed, no longer entire, from the rest of the tomb, from the asylum we might say of death, cutting them in pieces, rending them asunder.

Yet, banded together as we are, ever so ready to sacrifice our lives, what single case of revenge for injury are you able to point to, though, if it were held right among us to repay evil by evil, a single night with a torch or two could achieve an ample vengeance? But away with the idea of a sect divine avenging itself by human fires, or shrinking from the sufferings in which it is tried.

If we desired, indeed, to act the part of open enemies, not merely of secret avengers, would there be any lacking in strength, whether of numbers or resources? The Moors, the Marcomanni, the Parthians themselves, or any single people, however great, inhabiting a distinct territory, and confined within its own boundaries, surpasses, forsooth, in numbers, one spread over all the world! We are but of yesterday, and we have filled every place among you—cities, islands, fortresses, towns, market-places, the very camp, tribes, companies, palace, senate, forum—we have left nothing to you but the temples of your gods. For what wars should we not be fit, not eager, even with unequal forces, we who so willingly yield ourselves to the sword, if in our religion it were not counted better to be slain than to slay?

———

The third-century church needed to answer two questions. The first: How do we respond to persecution? The second: How do we counter false teaching?

The danger when the church faces opposition is that her responses mirror the tactics of those who are not Christians. We forget that the weapons of our warfare are spiritual (2 Cor. 10:4).

In the contemporary world, sometimes under the guise of "faithfulness," the shouted accusations and chants of secular humanists are met by a mirror-image response on the part of Christians. Turn down the sound on the TV, and the facial expressions become indistinguishable. It is the modern expression of the spirit that led Christians in the past to employ physical force and even military tactics to achieve spiritual ends. Our Lord said, "All who take the sword will perish by the sword" (Matt. 26:52). His words have a broad application, for He taught us that there is such a thing as attempted murder by words (Matt. 5:21–22). Spiritual warfare requires different artillery. We need to remember that "though we walk in the flesh, we are not waging war according to the flesh. For the weapons of our warfare are not of the flesh but have divine power to destroy strongholds" (2 Cor. 10:3–4). The early church, therefore, responded to opposition by expounding, defending, and living out the truth of the gospel.

We know relatively little about "ordinary" Christians in the early years of the church. But we do have access to the minds of a group of men known collectively as "the Apologists"—authors who expounded and defended the Christian faith. They were ready (in Simon Peter's words) to give "a defense [Greek *apologia*] to anyone who asks . . . for a reason for the hope that is in you" (1 Peter 3:15).

Justin Martyr

One such apologist in the second century was Flavius Justinus, more popularly known as Justin Martyr. Originally from Samaria, and having already tried various contemporary philosophical systems, Justin was one day walking along the shore when he met an elderly man who explained the gospel to him. Thereafter, he sought out Christians and devoted himself to itinerant evangelism. He wrote two volumes of apology for the Christian faith and is especially remembered for his *Dialogue* with a Jew by the name of Trypho. Around the year 166, a philosopher called Crescens, whom Justin had bettered in debate, plotted his arrest. With a number of others, Justin was scourged and executed.

Sometimes Christians have been accused of sacrificing their intellect. With Justin, the reverse was the case. Rather than sacrifice his intellect, since it had been persuaded of the truth of the gospel, Justin chose to sacrifice his life.

In the third century, two Christian thinkers emerged whose work was of lasting significance. They were both great men, although, like Justin, at best they were only men.

The first of these was Origen.

Origen of Alexandria

Born in Alexandria, Egypt, in 185, Origenes Adamantius was a prodigy. While he was still a teenager, his father, Leonidas, was arrested and imprisoned for his Christian faith. Already committed to the gospel, Origen wrote to his father, encouraging him not to deny his faith. By the time he was eighteen, he was serving as an instructor in theology. Over the next decade or so, he traveled widely and studied diligently in order to increase his usefulness. His fame spread as far as the emperor's family (Julia, the mother of the emperor Alexander Severus, even invited him to explain the Christian faith to her).

Origen lived by the most rigorous pattern of self-discipline and denial. On the one hand, he was attracted to excessive rigor (he seems to have taken Matt. 19:12 literally). On the other hand, this rigor, coupled with his imposing intellectual ability (and, doubtless, the reputation he had gained for both), engendered jealousy.

Origen's inquisitive and restless mind was drawn to speculative thinking. And although he tried to distinguish between the cardinal doctrines the church confessed and his own speculative theology, it is perhaps inevitable that he is usually remembered for the latter. He stands out as perhaps the most brilliant, but also the most adventurous, Christian thinker of the third century.

One of the questions with which he wrestled was, How do we go about reading the Bible, since it is a *sacred* book?

Origen lived in a culture still dominated by the presupposition that the material is inherently inferior to the spiritual and that the heavenly is the real and that the earthly, at best, is a poor imitation. In this context, when it came to reading sacred texts, the plain meaning (understanding the words and grammar in the light of their context) was viewed as inferior to the "spiritual" meaning. Thus, when Origen came to read the New Testament, he thought we should look for several levels or dimensions of significance in the text. Yes, there would be the natural meaning—the kind of meaning we would see in a book that is not sacred in any way. But then we must dig deeper and look for a moral and a spiritual meaning. At least on occasion, that meaning can be found only by interpreting the Bible in an allegorical way.

Origen inherited rather than invented this approach to reading texts, but in some ways he became the patron saint of Christians who are always looking for "deeper," hidden meanings. The net effect of this approach is that the really important thing to see in Scripture is not its grammatical sense but something that lies hidden within or under the surface. That, in many ways, had a harmful effect on the way in which the Bible was read for the next twelve centuries and beyond.

In addition, Origen was, as far as we know, the first Christian to attempt what we would call a coherent systematic theology. It was entitled *Peri archōn* (or, in the Latin translation that was edited and preserved, *De principiis*)—*On First Principles*. In four books, he expounded the doctrine of God, the creation and the incarnation, human freedom (the issue of determinism was a major one in his cultural context), and the doctrine of Scripture, rounding the whole work off with some comments on the Trinity.

In his theology, Origen boldly went where others dared not go. To be fair, he sought to distinguish between the centrality of the gospel the church confessed and the private views that he thought best explained Scripture. But it is the latter that tend to be remembered. He believed, for example, that the fall took place before the physical creation of man, and he found this view vindicated by the words of Psalm 119:67: "Before I was afflicted I went astray." He also held that the cosmic reconciliation effected by Christ implied that everyone—including the devil—would ultimately be saved. In addition, he bequeathed a form of subordination-ism to the church, which implied that the Father was actually the origin of the Son's deity. His speculative views were condemned at a synod in Constantinople in 543.[1]

Tertullian

The second individual whose influence lasted long beyond his own life-time was Quintus Septimius Florens Tertullianus, better known simply as Tertullian.

Born in Carthage, North Africa, around 160 or 170, Tertullian was brought up in a non-Christian home. By his own admission, he lived a profligate life until he was thirty or even older, when he was mastered by Christ. Perhaps against that background, it is not surprising that he was attracted to an ascetic lifestyle thereafter. He was, clearly, a man passion-ate to understand reality.

Tertullian wrestled with two major issues. First, Tertullian opposed a false doctrine of God the Trinity known as *modalism*—the view that there is one God, but He manifests Himself in three different modes, now as Father, then as Son, and then again as Holy Spirit. Thus, there are not three distinct persons but only three different manifestations of the One. The revelation of God is therefore like a one-man play: one actor plays all of the parts, appearing in different guises to perform different roles, and therefore never appearing simultaneously in all three roles.

Does it really matter how we think about the Trinity? After all, surely it is the most speculative—not to say the least practical—of all the doc-trines of the Christian faith?

That may well be the perspective of twenty-first-century Christians. But we modern Christians can sometimes exhibit an overweening ability to imitate the Corinthians and, comparing ourselves with ourselves, we assume we are "normal."[2] For such modalism, whether in the guise of ancient theology or modern indifference, destroys the New Testament's teaching about the inner fellowship of God as Father, Son, and Spirit. It ignores the realities described in the text of the New Testament, where the three are clearly distinguished from one another and all three are simultaneously present.[3] Moreover, it destroys the revelation we are given in Christ: the Father sending His Son to die for us and the Spirit being sent to bring us into union and communion with Christ. Remove the truth confessed in the church's doctrine of the Trinity, and the gospel itself unravels. Tertullian fought that tooth and nail. As far as we know, he was the first person in the history of the church to use the word *Trinity* (Latin *trinitas*), three-in-oneness, to summarize the New Testament teaching.

Tertullian's second problem was the growing moral laxity and spiritual indifference he witnessed in professing Christians. Yes, many continued to experience costly suffering for the cause of Christ. Yet, paradoxically, a new synthesis was emerging—a Christianity whose lukewarmness would not attract persecution. That problem is still with us. Many contemporary church members regard it as normal to be indifferent to worship, service, and witness while finding nothing strange in the expectation of organizations such as the local Rotary Club that members will be present at weekly meetings. Applied to church membership, such an expectation immediately raises the cry of "legalism!" Something, surely, has gone seriously wrong.

Hymn from the Apostolic Constitutions[4]

Praise ye the Lord, ye servants of the Lord;
Praise ye his name; his lordly honor sing;
Thee we adore; to thee glad homage bring;
Thee we acknowledge; God to be adored
For thy great glory, Sovereign, Lord, and King.
Father of Christ—of him whose work was done,
When by his death he took our sins away—
To thee belongeth worship, day by day,
Yea, holy Father, everlasting Son,
And Holy Ghost, all praise be thine for aye!

4

THE FOURTH CENTURY
A MOMENTOUS TIME

The name of Athanasius is permanently linked to the exposition and defense of the person of the Lord Jesus Christ. The following text is excerpted from Athanasius' On the Incarnation.

None, then, could bestow incorruption, but He Who had made, none restore the likeness of God, save His Own Image, none quicken, but the Life, none teach, but the Word. And He, to pay our debt of death, must also die for us, and rise again as our first-fruits from the grave. Mortal therefore His Body must be; corruptible, His Body could not be.

We have, then, now stated in part, as far as it was possible, and as ourselves had been able to understand, the reason of His bodily appearing; that it was in the power of none other to turn the corruptible to incorruption, except the Saviour Himself, that had at the beginning also made all things out of nought and that none other could create anew the likeness of God's image for men, save the Image of the Father; and that none other could render the mortal immortal, save our Lord Jesus Christ, Who is the Very Life; and that none other could teach men of the Father, and destroy the worship of idols, save the Word, that orders all things and is alone the true Only-begotten Son of the Father. But since it was necessary also that the debt owing from all should be paid again: for, as I have already said, it was owing that all should die, for which special cause, indeed, He came among us: to this intent, after the proofs of His Godhead from His works, He next offered up His sacrifice also on behalf of all, yielding His Temple to death in the stead of all, in order firstly to make men quit and free of their old trespass, and further to show Himself more powerful even than death, displaying His own body incorruptible, as first-fruits of the resurrection of all. And do not be surprised if we frequently repeat the same words on the same subject. For since we are speaking of the counsel of God, therefore we expound the same sense in more than one form, lest we should seem to be leaving anything out, and incur the charge of inadequate treatment: for it is better to submit to the blame of repetition than to leave out anything that ought to be set down. The body, then, as sharing the same nature with all, for it was a human body, though by an unparalleled miracle it was formed of a virgin only, yet being mortal, was to die also, conformably to its peers. But by virtue of the union of the Word with it, it was no longer subject to corruption according to its own nature, but by reason of the Word that had come to dwell in it was placed out of the reach of corruption. And so it was that two marvels came to pass at once, that the death of all was accomplished in the Lord's body, and that death and corruption were wholly done away by reason of the Word that was united with it. For there was need of death, and death must needs be suffered on behalf of all, that the debt owing from all might be paid. Whence, as I said before, the Word, since it was not possible for Him to die, as He was immortal, took to Himself a body such as could die, that He might offer it as His own in the stead of all, and as suffering, through His union with it, on behalf of all, bring to nought him that had the power of death, that is the devil; and might deliver them who through fear of death were all their lifetime subject to bondage.

———

The fourth century was one of the most significant periods in the first fifteen hundred years of the church's existence. In it, a number of events took place that set the trajectory of the church into the future.

The century opened with two important developments.

Persecution

Christians are called to live at peace with others in society (see Rom. 12:18). But despite the church's desire to contribute to society and live at peace, persecution continues. Rarely do emperors or dictators grasp the fact that Christians will be their very best citizens. Tragically, rulers often see totalitarianism as preferable to grace and its effects.

When the century opened, Diocletian (245–313) had already been Roman emperor for a decade and a half. Born in obscurity, he rose through the ranks of the military and was declared emperor in 284. He was an extraordinarily gifted organizer and administrator and in his own way a reformer of the now-unstable empire. For the major part of his reign, Christians enjoyed relative peace. But Diocletian became convinced that the only way the Roman Empire could be strengthened was by virtually totalitarian rule. This in turn required a commitment on the part of every citizen to his "divine" authority as *sacratissimus Dominus noster* (our most sacred Lord). Anything that stood in the way of this grand plan was repressed.

In 303, persecution broke out, and churches were destroyed. Realizing that Christianity was a book-anchored faith, Diocletian also sought to destroy Christians' books, especially the Scriptures. Then he sought to destroy the leaders of the church, and eventually Christians in general, if they refused to bow to his decree that all citizens of the empire must make sacrifices to the gods of Rome. By God's grace, many Christians had the courage to stand firm.

Diocletian abdicated in 305 and lived out the closing years of his life in retirement at what is now Split, Croatia. But the persecution continued.

It is sometimes difficult to distinguish truth from exaggeration when we read accounts of martyrdoms. At times, they appear exaggerated. But perhaps the exaggeration grew out of a desire to draw a contrast with other Christians who were intimidated, some of whom handed over copies of the Scriptures that were burned. This led to a new problem for the church, namely, failed Christians, the *traditores*. What if in later times of relative ease they wanted to return to the fold?

Diocletian took his own life in 313. Two years earlier, the Edict of Nicomedia (311) had brought the persecution to an end.

The Cult of Softness[1]

The sufferings endured by so many Christians highlighted a second trend: an increasing sense of ease and comfort in those who professed to be the followers of the crucified One.

There are mysteries in the Christian faith and doctrines that stretch the mind. But sometimes it is not the revelation that stretches reason to the full but the teaching that is simplest and clearest that presents the greatest challenges. We trust and follow a crucified Savior raised from the dead. Consequently, our lives will be marked by the cross. The way to life is the way of death.

Since we naturally draw back from suffering, it should not surprise us if the same reaction was present at the beginning of the fourth century.

One response to the "subtle love of softening things"[2] made by not a few was to reject the world, to abandon society and to live as hermits,[3] distanced from the world and separated from worldly Christians. This movement gained strength especially in Egypt as men moved out into the desert to live totally solitary lives, contemplating (as they hoped) the glories of God and seeking His presence and power to overcome temptation. Many of them discovered, however, that the desert is also territory that the devil occupies.

Antony

The most influential of these hermits was Antony (251–356), who was born in Coma, Egypt. While at a church service shortly after the death of his parents, he was gripped by Jesus' words to the rich young ruler telling him to sell everything and follow Him. Taking the words literally, he committed himself to an ascetic desert lifestyle from around 285 until 305, when he organized a group of monks. Later, he returned to the desert. He was widely admired, especially when the *Life of Antony* (written by Athanasius) became popular.

Paradoxically, both of these influences—persecution and monasticism—had the potential to destroy the witness of Christians. If either the darkness overcomes the light or the light is removed from the world, the world goes dark. If we take the salt out of the world, moral and spiritual decay is inevitable. These desert monks, then, despite their remarkable asceticism, stand as a warning to us that Christ has called us not to leave the world but to live sacrificially in it.

Besides these movements, we should take note of three significant events that took place during the fourth century.

Constantine

The first was that *Constantine became the emperor*. According to the fourth-century Christian author Lactantius,[4] as Constantine fought for control of the Roman Empire, he had a remarkable dream just before the Battle of Milvian Bridge.[5] As a result, he fought under the sign of the cross, which became the famous *chi-rho* monogram (from the first two letters in the title *Christ*). Whatever the truth may be, Constantine won the battle, and he attributed his victory to the power of Christ. Immediately, he began to relax the penal laws against Christians and eventually made Christianity the official religion of the great Roman Empire.

That was good news—the end of persecution. But it was also bad news. It was good news in the sense that Christians were now free to worship Christ without physical hindrance. But it was bad news in the sense that for the first time, Christianity became the state religion. Citizens of the Roman Empire would now view themselves as de facto Christians. The basic biblical distinction between natural birth and spiritual birth was lost. Constantine did much to help the church. But this fatal mistake hindered the church in the long term by minimizing the difference between a citizen of this world and a citizen of the world to come. The church in the West has never been quite the same since then.

Nicaea

The second major event of the fourth century was the *Council of Nicaea* in 325. It officially (but not finally) settled a bitter debate in the church on the identity of Christ.

The seeds of this debate can be found in the way early Christian writers answered the question, In what sense is Christ fully divine? The issue came to a head through the teaching of a presbyter (minister) by the name of Arius,[6] who had argued that if the Son was, as the church confessed, "begotten of the Father," then "there was a time when the Son was not."

Over against Arius stood the heroic figure of Athanasius.[7] He argued powerfully that if the Son is not Himself fully God, then He cannot reconcile us to God since His death would not have infinite power to save us from sin against an infinite and holy God. Only if Christ is fully divine can He reconcile us to God. Furthermore, Athanasius argued, if Christ is not truly God (and by implication, the same would be true of the Holy Spirit), then Christians are baptized in the name of one God and two of His creatures. In other words, the inaugural Christian rite of baptism into the one name of the Father, the Son, and the Holy Spirit requires the full deity of the Son in order to make sense.

For his dogged faithfulness, Athanasius (nicknamed "The Black Dwarf" because of his coloring and height) was exiled on no fewer than five occasions. But even if the whole world was against him, he was determined to uphold the full deity of his Savior (hence the expression *Athanasius contra mundum*, "Athanasius against the world"). The council that Constantine summoned at Nicaea in 325 confirmed Athanasius' New Testament conviction about the absolute deity of our Lord Jesus Christ.

Augustine

A third major event of the fourth century took place in the life of an individual whose writings have made him the single most influential thinker in the church since the days of the Apostles. The event was, of course, *the conversion of Augustine.*

Aurelius Augustinus was born in 354 in Thagaste, North Africa (Annaba in modern-day Algeria), the son of a pagan father and a Christian mother, Monica (to whose prayers Augustine later partly attributed his conversion). New thinking and envelope-pushing experiences fascinated him. At the age of eighteen, he took a concubine with whom he lived for the next fifteen years. He seems to have tried everything, including new religion and even extraordinary diets (at one time he belonged to a sect that believed that you should eat as many melons as you could).

He found no satisfaction. Writing about his experience in his most famous work, *The Confessions,* he notes that however much he sought what he thought was the truth, he was really running away from it and from the grace of God in Jesus Christ.

Eventually, Augustine took a prestigious job as a professor of rhetoric in Milan, Italy. He began to listen to the preaching of the great Ambrose, bishop of Milan. One day, as he sat in a garden, he heard a child in a neighboring garden shouting out some words he thought were part of a game—*tolle lege* (pick up and read). It triggered something in his mind. He picked up a copy of the New Testament that was lying on a table and opened it at Romans 13:14: "But put on the Lord Jesus Christ, and make no provision for the flesh, to gratify its desires." He felt that God had spoken to him as directly as he had heard the child's voice. He did exactly what the text said. He trusted in Christ. The old way of life was now gone. He found the rest in God for which he then knew he had been created. From then on, he would be the devoted servant of Jesus Christ. His thinking and writing in many ways determined the course of the history of Christian theology, right through to the Reformation.

One of the most fascinating statements in *The Confessions* is a comment Augustine made about Ambrose. He was describing the time in his life when he came to Milan. What was it that impressed him about the bishop? He tells us in his prayer-soliloquy to God: "I began to like him, at first indeed not as a teacher of the truth, for I had absolutely no confidence in your Church, *but as a human being who was kind to me. . . .* Nevertheless, gradually, though I did not realize it, I was drawing closer."[8]

We have seen that Justin Martyr was brought to Christ by an otherwise unknown elderly Christian taking a quiet walk along the shore; Augustine came to faith through an eloquent bishop's kindness and a mother's prayers. Justin's name lives on in the history of the church—but the old man who pointed him to Christ is forgotten. Many Christians are familiar with the name of Augustine. Fewer know the name of his mother or the name of his minister, Ambrose.

There is a pattern and a lesson here. As we read the lives of men and women who have been strategically used by Christ in building His kingdom, we note that the names of those through whom they were brought to faith in Jesus Christ are often forgotten or lost. But their significance is incalculable. God delights to use the hidden and the forgotten.

This is, surely, a tremendous encouragement to people like us who live our Christian lives in relative obscurity. We do not expect to find our names in any church history book. And yet, it may be that someone to whom we are kind because we love Jesus will be taken up and extraordinarily used by God to build the church of Jesus Christ.

Faithfulness is far more significant than fame when Jesus is building His church.

Saviour of the Nations, Come

AMBROSE OF MILAN (C. 339–97)[9]

Saviour of the nations, come,
Virgin's Son, here make Thy home!
Marvel now, O heaven and earth,
That the Lord chose such a birth.

Not by human flesh and blood;
By the Spirit of our God
Was the Word of God made flesh,
Woman's offspring, pure and fresh.

Wondrous birth! O wondrous Child
Of the virgin undefiled!
Though by all the world disowned,
Still to be in heaven enthroned.

From the Father forth He came
And returneth to the same,
Captive leading death and hell
High the song of triumph swell!

Thou, the Father's only Son,
Hast over sin the victory won.
Boundless shall Thy kingdom be;
When shall we its glories see?

Brightly doth Thy manger shine,
Glorious is its light divine.
Let not sin o'ercloud this light;
Ever be our faith thus bright.

Praise to God the Father sing,
Praise to God the Son, our King,
Praise to God the Spirit be
Ever and eternally.

5

THE FIFTH CENTURY

GOD'S SOVEREIGNTY
OVER ALL

This moving account written by Patrick helps us get behind the legend to the heart of the man himself. It is excerpted from Patrick's **Confession.**

I, Patrick, a sinner, a most simple countryman, the least of all the faithful and most contemptible to many, had for father the deacon Calpurnius, son of the late Potitus, a priest, of the settlement of Bannavem Taburniae; he had a small villa nearby where I was taken captive. I was at that time about sixteen years of age. I did not, indeed, know the true God; and I was taken into captivity in Ireland with many thousands of people, according to our deserts, for quite drawn away from God, we did not keep his precepts, nor were we obedient to our priests who used to remind us of our salvation. And the Lord brought down on us the fury of his being and scattered us among many nations, even to the ends of the earth, where I, in my smallness, am now to be found among foreigners.

And there the Lord opened my mind to an awareness of my unbelief, in order that, even so late, I might remember my transgressions and turn with all my heart to the Lord my God, who had regard for my insignificance and pitied my youth and ignorance. And he watched over me before I knew him, and before I learned sense or even distinguished between good and evil, and he protected me, and consoled me as a father would his son.

Therefore, indeed, I cannot keep silent, nor would it be proper, so many favours and graces has the Lord deigned to bestow on me in the land of my captivity. For after chastisement from God, and recognizing him, our way to repay him is to exalt him and confess his wonders before every nation under heaven.

For there is no other God, nor ever was before, nor shall be here-after, but God the Father, unbegotten and without beginning, in whom all things began, whose are all things, as we have been taught; and his son Jesus Christ, who manifestly always existed with the Father, before the beginning of time in the spirit with the Father, indescribably begotten before all things, and all things visible and invisible were made by him. He was made man, conquered death and was received into Heaven, to the Father who gave him all power over every name in Heaven and on Earth and in Hell, so that every tongue should confess that Jesus Christ is Lord and God, in whom we believe. And we look to his imminent coming again, the judge of the living and the dead, who will render to each according to his deeds. And he poured out his Holy Spirit on us in abundance, the gift and pledge of immortality, which makes the believers and the obedient into sons of God and co-heirs of Christ who is revealed, and we worship one God in the Trinity of holy name.

———

The teaching of Augustine, bishop of Hippo Regius, runs like a brightly colored thread through church history. His life straddles the fourth and fifth centuries and is connected in significant ways with two major moments that left their mark on the Christian church.

The Fall of Rome

The first of these was *the sack of Rome*. The once inconceivable became a reality (how often that error of judgment has been repeated) on August 24, 410, at the hands of the Visigoths, but it had been coming for some time. For the previous several decades, the "barbarian" Germanic tribes had been making military advances. In 430, another Germanic tribe, the Vandals, reached the gates of Hippo Regius, as Augustine lay dying.

Disaster often leads to the knee-jerk reaction of seeking a scapegoat. It was no different in the early fifth century. In this instance, Rome's demise was blamed on Christians and their God—it was a judgment for the Christians' rejection of the ancient gods. In some senses, this was a mass political form of a common instinct in the natural man's heart: when things are going well, God is not praised, nor is His intervention in life desired or loved. But when things go badly wrong, people complain about His lack of sovereign intervention. Now, in the early fifth century, the church became the scapegoat for the tragedy that befell the empire.

It was to this false view of history that Augustine responded in his famous work *The City of God.* This large and very great book has a simple theme: from the beginning of history, two cities have been in the process of building—the City of Man and the City of God. Both cities are built on love. But these loves are antithetical: the City of Man is built on the love of self (*amor sui*); the City of God is built on the love of God (*amor Dei*).

God has sovereignly permitted man to build his empires, but there is only one kingdom that lasts—the *regnum Dei*, the kingdom of God. All others are transient; they rise and fall. But the kingdom that God is building in Jesus Christ, the City of God, the church, will never perish. And so Augustine's message for his fellow Christians was, in essence:

This is no surprise to us. The Church was promised ongoing conflict from Genesis 3:15 to the end. We expect to see the kingdoms of men rising and then falling, and the "seed of the serpent" seeking to crush the "seed of the woman." Christians are committed to "the eternal city." But it is not Rome. Our commitment is to Jesus Christ and his church. There are always two kingdoms, two cities, and two kings. But only the city of God and of King Jesus will last forever.

Augustine thus emphasized the sovereignty of God's grace on the large canvas of history. That message is a fundamental one for Christians in every time period. It is the message of Matthew 16:18. It is the message given dramatic expression in the book of Revelation. God is sovereign in human history.

Pelagianism

The second moment was *the Pelagian Controversy*.

Augustine emphasized the sovereignty of God not only in history in general but also in redemption in particular. Given his own story, he could not but believe in the sovereign grace of God. But he found that this simply agreed with biblical, and especially Pauline, emphases. As a result, he found himself involved in a major theological controversy that has continued to echo through the centuries.[1]

Pelagius (c. 354–418) was a British monk whose outward life was marked by rigorous self-discipline and personal piety. His ministry was set within the context of lax Christian profession. He therefore found himself disturbed by some words in Augustine's famous autobiographical *Confessions*: "My entire hope is exclusively in your very great mercy. Grant what you command, and command what you will [*da quod iubes, et iube quod vis*]."[2]

Augustine was saying, in essence, "Lord, You are sovereign and You may command anything that pleases You, but we are not able to accomplish what You command. You tell us to obey Your Word and will, but we are sinners and we cannot. So, give us obedience. You tell us to have

faith in Jesus Christ. We try to do this, but we can neither obey You as You desire nor trust You as we should. Since we are unable of ourselves to trust in Jesus Christ, by Your sovereign grace help us to trust in and obey Him."

Pelagius rejected this "miserable sinner Christianity" (as it would later come to be known). He felt that it undermined human responsibility. As a result, he downplayed the impact of original sin and total depravity. After all, had he not himself achieved considerable levels of devotion and obedience? By contrast, Augustine emphasized that it is only by God's grace that we are able to trust and obey. Grace, he understood, not only undermines self-sufficiency but also pride. Our righteousness is as filthy rags, as is our sinfulness (Isa. 64:6). Yet this does not destroy human responsibility; in fact, the very reverse is true: grace makes faith and obedience possible. Thus, Augustine developed a famous schema to describe the human condition:[3]

- In the state of innocence, man was capable of not sinning (*posse non peccare*), but also capable of sinning (*posse peccare*).
- In the state of sin, man is not capable of not sinning (*non posse non peccare*).
- In the state of regeneration, man becomes capable of not sinning (*posse non peccare*) yet remains capable of sinning (*posse peccare*).
- In the state of glory, man becomes incapable of sinning at all (*non posse peccare*).

Augustine clarified the biblical teaching in a series of anti-Pelagian writings.

Behind this controversy lay the question of the basis and foundation of our justification. Is it exclusively in Christ, or do we somehow contribute to it? Thanks to the enormous biblical learning and perseverance of Augustine, the teaching of Pelagius was (at least formally) marginalized in the Christian church.[4]

Yet, alas, the church would later dilute and weaken the full-blooded teaching of Augustine in various mutations of Pelagianism. The Princeton theologian Charles Hodge would later say that he was more afraid of the ghost of semi-Pelagius than he was of Pelagius. Semi-Pelagius is the ghost that hovers around every person who believes that "heaven helps those who help themselves" or that justification is achieved by outweighing sins with good deeds. In all its various guises, it is a theology that remains one of the major enemies of Christ's gospel. By contrast, Augustine saw clearly that the gospel teaches that we are dead in sin, not merely sick or weak (Eph. 2:1). We therefore cannot please God. The only hope we have of standing in God's presence is if in Jesus Christ He shows us His saving grace and draws us out of our darkness into His marvelous light (1 Peter 2:9).

Christianity in Britain

References to Pelagius as a "British" monk alert us to the fact that by this time the Christian gospel had already come to what we now call "the British Isles."

Exactly how it did so remains unclear. It probably came first through members of the invading Roman military. In all likelihood, merchants and businessmen traveling throughout the Roman Empire brought word of the new faith. Certainly by the end of the third century, there were churches in England. And around the mid- to late fifth century, Patrick began to preach the gospel.

Patrick

Scholars have long debated Patrick's origins. He himself tells us that he was born in Banna Venta Berniae.[5] His mother seems to have been closely related to the famous bishop Martin of Tours (c. 316–97).

In his early life, Patrick was captured by Irish pirates, was sold to a sheep farmer, and became a shepherd. He comments on the fact that although he had been brought up in a Christian home, he was not a Christian himself. He was a stranger to the living God. But during these years of slavery, he believed God had visited him and opened his heart to the gospel. In his early twenties, he escaped and devoted himself to a life of Christian service.

Sometime later, Patrick had his own "Macedonian call"—a visionary experience of some kind. In it, a man named Victoricus from Ireland gave him a letter headed "The Voice of the Irish." As he began to read it, he felt that he was being called by the people of Ireland, who cried out to him, "We appeal to you, holy servant boy, come and walk among us!" He returned to Ireland and labored ceaselessly in spreading, and encouraging others to spread, the gospel message. Thereafter, he seems to have baptized thousands of people and was instrumental in conversions among the wealthy and noble.

Over the centuries, a wide variety of myths and legends have grown up about Patrick (as with many Christian leaders in this period). It is indeed difficult even for scholars to separate the wheat from the chaff. But it is noteworthy how Patrick describes himself—"Patrick, an unlearned man and a sinner." There is an Apostolic ring to that confession.

Patrick stands as a testimony to the way in which God plucks men and women not only out of total obscurity but often out of conditions of physical difficulty (in his case, slavery) and forms them into sharp weapons in His hands. He subdues them to Himself, wastes no experience, molds them for His purposes, and then channels them in some special way to become servants of Christ. Thankfully, the history of the Christian church is punctuated by such men and women. Some have come from backgrounds of great privilege, but many more have had their roots in total obscurity and often deprivation.

So, what do these portraits from the fifth century teach us?

They teach us that the kingdoms man builds never last. The only lasting kingdom is the kingdom of Jesus Christ.

They teach us that salvation is not by our own accomplishment but by grace alone through faith in Jesus Christ. That is the gospel.

They teach us that the Lord delights to take people from obscure backgrounds, training them by trying circumstances and employing them in His service in the City of God.

These are lessons we need to learn just as much in the twenty-first century as Augustine and Patrick did in the fifth century.

Of the Father's Love Begotten

AURELIUS CLEMENS PRUDENTIUS (348–413)

Of the Father's love begotten, ere the worlds began to be,
He is Alpha and Omega, He the source, the ending He,
Of the things that are, that have been,
And that future years shall see, evermore and evermore!

At His Word the worlds were framèd; He commanded; it was done:
Heaven and earth and depths of ocean in their threefold order one;
All that grows beneath the shining
Of the moon and burning sun, evermore and evermore!

He is found in human fashion, death and sorrow here to know,
That the race of Adam's children doomed by law to endless woe,
May not henceforth die and perish
In the dreadful gulf below, evermore and evermore!

O that birth forever blessèd, when the virgin, full of grace,
By the Holy Ghost conceiving, bare the Saviour of our race;
And the Babe, the world's Redeemer,
First revealed His sacred face, evermore and evermore!

This is He Whom seers in old time chanted of with one accord;
Whom the voices of the prophets promised in their faithful word;
Now He shines, the long expected,
Let creation praise its Lord, evermore and evermore!

O ye heights of heaven adore Him; angel hosts, His praises sing;
Powers, dominions, bow before Him, and extol our God and King!
Let no tongue on earth be silent,
Every voice in concert sing, evermore and evermore!

Righteous judge of souls departed, righteous King of them that live,
On the Father's throne exalted none in might with Thee may strive;

Who at last in vengeance coming
Sinners from Thy face shalt drive, evermore and evermore!

Thee let old men, thee let young men, thee let boys in chorus sing;
Matrons, virgins, little maidens, with glad voices answering:
Let their guileless songs re-echo,
And the heart its music bring, evermore and evermore!

Christ, to Thee with God the Father, and, O Holy Ghost, to Thee,
Hymn and chant with high thanksgiving, and unwearied praises be:
Honor, glory, and dominion,
And eternal victory, evermore and evermore!

THE SIXTH CENTURY

CHRISTIANITY IN SCOTLAND

The most famous rule of the monastic orders was written by Benedict (480–547), the founder of the Benedictines. It contains seventy-three chapters. Below, he describes the "good works" of the monk. His counsels provide an illustration of the ideal of monastic godliness. It is of interest to compare them with the resolutions of Jonathan Edwards in chapter 18.

Chapter IV: The Instruments of Good Works

(1) In the first place to love the Lord God with the whole heart, the whole soul, the whole strength . . .

(2) Then, one's neighbour as one's self (cf. Matt. 22:37–39; Mark 12:30–31; Luke 10:27).

(3) Then, not to kill . . . (4) Not to commit adultery . . . (5) Not to steal . . . (6) Not to covet (cf. Rom. 13:9).

(7) Not to bear false witness (cf. Matt. 19:18; Mark 10:19; Luke 18:20). (8) To honor all men (cf. 1 Peter 2:17).

(9) And what one would not have done to himself, not to do to another (cf. Tobit 4:16; Matt. 7:12; Luke 6:31).

(10) To deny one's self in order to follow Christ (cf. Matt. 16:24;

Luke 9:23). (11) To chastise the body (cf. 1 Cor. 9:27). (12) Not to seek after pleasures. (13) To love fasting. (14) To relieve the poor. (15) To clothe the naked. (16) To visit the sick (cf. Matt. 25:36). (17) To bury the dead. (18) To help in trouble. (19) To console the sorrowing. (20) To hold one's self aloof from worldly ways. (21) To prefer nothing to the love of Christ.

(22) Not to give way to anger. (23) Not to foster a desire for revenge.

(24) Not to entertain deceit in the heart. (25) Not to make a false peace.

(26) Not to forsake charity. (27) Not to swear, lest perchance one swear falsely.

(28) To speak the truth with heart and tongue. (29) Not to return evil for evil (cf. 1 Thess. 5:15; 1 Peter 3:9).

(30) To do no injury, yea, even patiently to bear the injury done us. (31) To love one's enemies (cf. Matt. 5:44; Luke 6:27).

(32) Not to curse them that curse us, but rather to bless them. (33) To bear persecution for justice' sake (cf. Matt. 5:10).

(34) Not to be proud . . . (35) Not to be given to wine (cf. Titus 1:7; 1 Tim. 3:3).

(36) Not to be a great eater. (37) Not to be drowsy. (38) Not to be slothful (cf. Rom. 12:11). (39) Not to be a murmurer. (40) Not to be a detractor. (41) To put one's trust in God.

(42) To refer what good one sees in himself, not to self, but to God.

(43) But as to any evil in himself, let him be convinced that it is his own and charge it to himself.

(44) To fear the day of judgment. (45) To be in dread of hell.

(46) To desire eternal life with all spiritual longing. (47) To keep death before one's eyes daily.

(48) To keep a constant watch over the actions of our life. (49) To hold as certain that God sees us everywhere.

(50) To dash at once against Christ the evil thoughts which rise in one's heart.

(51) And to disclose them to our spiritual father. (52) To guard one's tongue against bad and wicked speech.

(53) Not to love much speaking. (54) Not to speak useless words and such as provoke laughter.

(55) Not to love much or boisterous laughter. (56) To listen willingly to holy reading.

(57) To apply one's self often to prayer. (58) To confess one's past sins to God daily in prayer with sighs and tears, and to amend them for the future.

(59) Not to fulfil the desires of the flesh (cf. Gal. 5:16). (60) To hate one's own will.

(61) To obey the commands of the Abbot in all things, even though he himself (which Heaven forbid) act otherwise, mindful of that precept of the Lord: "What they say, do ye; what they do, do ye not" (Matt. 23:3).

(62) Not to desire to be called holy before one is; but to be holy first, that one may be truly so called.

(63) To fulfil daily the commandments of God by works. (64) To love chastity.

(65) To hate no one. (66) Not to be jealous; not to entertain envy.

(67) Not to love strife. (68) Not to love pride. (69) To honor the aged. (70) To love the younger.

(71) To pray for one's enemies in the love of Christ. (72) To make peace with an adversary before the setting of the sun. (73) And never to despair of God's mercy.

Behold, these are the instruments of the spiritual art, which, if they have been applied without ceasing day and night and approved on judgment day, will merit for us from the Lord that reward which He hath promised: "The eye hath not seen, nor the ear heard, neither hath it entered into the heart of man, what things God hath prepared for them that love Him" (1 Cor. 2:9). But the workshop in which we perform all these works with diligence is the enclosure of the monastery, and stability in the community.

Throughout the English-speaking world, Christians often, and rightly, associate the spread of the gospel with the Scottish church. Certainly, in much later centuries, the impact of the gospel in this small country would spread not only in the inventiveness of its native sons but in the passion for world evangelism that gripped many of its best believers. So, as we reach the sixth century, it is time to say something about the origins of Christian faith there.

Christianity in Scotland

We know very little about how Christ began to build His church in Scotland before the sixth century. As we have seen, God loves to do things in obscurity. The incarnation and early years of our Lord's life underscore that principle. The One who created the heavens and the earth out of nothing has no need of publicity.

Perhaps the most common contemporary image of pre-Reformation Scotland is the depiction of the primitive face-painted early-fourteenth-century warriors of the movie *Braveheart*. It may not be an altogether unfair representation. The nether regions of the country (*ultima thule* to the Romans) were, until long after that date, viewed as beyond the borders of civilization. Much of the region had never been subdued by the Romans, although in the first century the Roman governor Agricola did send his fleet to sail around the coast to make sure Britain was in fact an island. His son-in-law (the author Tacitus) described in his *Vita Agricolae* (Life of Agricola) the moderate climate of the islands but seemed particularly fascinated by the weather (nothing has changed since).[1]

What we now call Scotland was then essentially a land of four warring tribes: the Picts (*picti,* painted ones), who inhabited large tracts of Scotland north of the River Forth; the Angles, who lived between the River Forth and the River Humber; Britons in the west, whose activity centered on Dumbarton, from where they ruled over the region surrounding the River Clyde (Strathclyde); and the Scots, who (somewhat confusingly) were of Irish descent and had invaded the west of Scotland at the beginning of the sixth century.

The country was characterized by paganism. Druid-like figures ruled in many parts. It was (as it is today) a country in need of the power of the gospel. That gospel came largely through two individuals: Ninian and Columba.

Ninian

Few details are known about Ninian. In fact, historians are not absolutely certain in what century he lived. He brought the gospel to the southwest of Scotland, to the region of Whithorn (where he had, unusually, built a church using stone—the White House, or *candida cassa*), with which his name has ever since been linked. He gathered a small number of monks around him and created a community. Then, by means of duplicating these little communities, he evangelized the Picts, apparently with considerable success. Indeed, the view has sometimes been expressed that the single most significant event in the history of Scotland was the conversion of the Picts.

Ninian and his companions were evangelists—missionary monks. To some readers, that will seem to be a contradiction in terms.

Monk-Evangelists?

Evangelical Christians have almost always found the notion of monasticism either curious or repugnant, and even irreconcilable with the gospel. We think of monks as world-withdrawing rather than gospel-spreading. But these early monks in the Celtic tradition should be seen in a somewhat different light. Think of the best of them as men who devoted themselves to spreading the gospel. And remember that some forms of monasticism were virtual equivalents of a modern missionary society that believed fulfilling its vision required the commitment of single-minded young men willing to forgo the privileges and also the limitations of married life.[2]

Celtic monastic life at its best saw itself as an echo of the Apostolic pattern of church planting, albeit colored by the later history and shape of the church. It was built on the significant dual principle that building the church lies at the heart of Christ's vision and that the church as a community is His chief evangelistic agent.[3] Thus, the founding of a

monastic community in any area was a form of church planting. It func-
tioned as the equivalent of a missionary compound with its doors open
to the surrounding community.

The approach of Ninian, therefore, was to develop "gospel cells"
in places where there was no Christian witness. Gospel proclamation
accompanied by Christlike service and gospel lifestyle—illustrated by
the community of the saints living and working together—were the twin
engines that drove this mission-minded strategy. In fact, many monastic
cells were probably more deeply rooted in the community they sought to
reach than were some "missionary compounds" in later centuries.

Ninian had grasped a deep-seated element in the Apostolic evangelistic strategy: every Christian is a witness to Jesus Christ. But in the New
Testament, "witness" is less a specific activity and more a state of being,
set within the context of the life of the church as a community. Jesus sent
the Apostles to *be* witnesses rather than to "*do* witnessing." It is not the
occasional act of isolated individuals. In fact, in the New Testament we
read relatively little of the witness of *individual* Christians.

The New Testament letters were largely addressed to their readers
in the second person ("you") plural. Understandably, our English Bible
translations rarely indicate this. It would be ungainly to read a text constantly punctuated by "you (s.)" and "you (pl.)."[4] But it would underline
that the instructions and exhortations of the New Testament are usually
addressed to "you (pl.)." All that each of us is called to be in Christ is
what we are meant to be together, in fellowship with one another, not as
isolated individuals.

As Luke conducted his research for the Acts of the Apostles, he clearly
noticed this pattern. Thus, while four individuals feature largely in his
narrative (Peter, Philip, Stephen, and Paul), he also provides a series of
snapshots periodically illustrating the growth, spiritual condition, and
impact of the church as a community (Acts 1:12–15; 2:41; 2:47; 5:14;
6:1; 6:7; 9:31; 12:24; 16:5; 19:20).

One of the most telling of these passages is found in the paradoxical
statement he makes about the Jerusalem church in Acts 5: "*None of the rest
dared join them*, but the people held them in high esteem. *And more than*

ever believers were added to the Lord, multitudes of both men and women" (Acts 5:13–14, emphasis added). These statements seem at odds with one another. How can it be that, on the one hand, people did not dare to join the early Christians, and on the other hand, held them in high esteem? And how can people not dare to join, while more and more people are joining?

Luke sees this as an illustration of the church's living in the power and grace of the Spirit. The paradox is a hallmark of a living fellowship of God's people. Even while the costliness of commitment to Christ makes outsiders draw back with a deep sense of being unworthy or fearful, there is nevertheless something overwhelmingly attractive about the new community that makes being part of it so desirable. It is not unusual for an individual to hate or despise the convictions Christians share, only to find that there is a compelling integrity and "rightness" in their lives and especially in their fellowship with each other. Only the powerful presence of Christ explains this. How very different from the vision that has often dominated thinking about church life, worship, and evangelism in our own day!

This is altogether in tune with our Lord's prayer on the eve of His passion: "I do not ask for these only [the Apostles], but also for those who will believe in me through their word [all Christians in the future], that they may all be one, just as you, Father, are in me, and I in you, that they also may be in us, *so that the world may believe that you have sent me*" (John 17:20–21, emphasis added).

Interestingly, the strategy of Celtic monasticism was less "monastic" than the strategy of many church-builders in our own time who insist on building new (and usually larger) buildings as near to the junctions of major highways as possible rather than embedding them in the community. The reason? So that people can *travel from considerable distances* in order to be present on a *Sunday morning.*

The result? The church makes all too little impact on its neighborhood since its members neither live nor work there. And no one expects the congregation to come back again for a second service in the afternoon or evening of the Lord's Day. It would be too inconvenient.

This staggering lack of foresight and relative indifference to the wisdom of past generations leads in turn to such banal convictions (often fostered by specialist organizations of experts on church life) that "the quality of our morning worship is outstanding." But the only one capable of evaluating the quality of our worship of God is God Himself. So it is presumably performance and enjoyment that are being measured. If the wrong metrics are employed, the results are inevitably an illusion.

In fact, the acid test for the quality of worship in a congregation is the desire to worship the Lord more and to feed on His Word and sacraments more—and preferably soon. Historically, that has meant an afternoon or evening service. After all, the test a young woman employs for the quality of a date with a young man is not that after an hour she looks at her watch, fiddles with her smartphone, gets up to leave, and suggests it would be nice to do this again for an hour on the same day next week. No, she wants more time with this young man as soon as possible. Should the Bride of Christ treat her Betrothed with any less enthusiasm? Alas for our churches if we despise the wisdom of the past in the mistaken conviction that we know better and are the stronger Christians as a result. The evidence seems to point in the opposite direction.

But this is symptomatic of something else. When we build churches in locations where few of the members actually live, it should not surprise us therefore that *as communities* our churches often make little impact in the context in which they are set.

So there is more to learn from the ancient evangelistic strategies of these monks than meets the eye. Nor should we forget the Reformation view that Christians should live with the same kind of devotion and discipline in the church family and in the world as these men did in their distinctive communities.

The pattern that was exemplified in Ninian was further developed by Columba (or Colmcille, "the Dove of the Church"). He is a better-known figure because of the *Life of Columba*, which his friend and successor Adamnan wrote.

Columba

Columba (521–97) probably came from the region of Donegal in Ireland. He had already founded other monasteries[5] when, around midlife, as an act of penance,[6] he came with a small group of monks to the tiny island of Iona off the west coast of Scotland and established a monastery. This band of brothers devoted themselves to prayer, to the study of Scripture, to serving one another, and especially to creating a community of deep Christian commitment. It grew until the community numbered well over a hundred.

Then Columba began his great task of evangelizing the rest of Scotland.

We have grown accustomed to rapid transit, whether locally, nationally, or internationally. It is difficult for us to grasp the level of commitment itinerant evangelists displayed in the first millennium. Travel was hazardous at the best of times. There were no passports with inbuilt requests for their bearers to have safe passage, no foreign embassies to help in an emergency. In sixth-century Scotland, roads were virtually nonexistent. Yet from the Isle of Lewis in the northwest of Scotland down to Wigton in the southwest, over to the east coast around Aberdeenshire, and up to the northeast of Scotland and the outlying Orkney Islands, these little cell groups spread. They brought the name of Christ, and in the process found themselves engaged in spiritual warfare with paganism. They established themselves in the community and sought to preach and to illustrate the power of Christ's gospel.

Thus the gospel spread throughout Scotland. Doubtless, many of the traditions that developed around Ninian and Columba, as well as Kentigern (Mungo)[7] and other well-known Scottish "saints," are exaggerated hagiography. It is not easy to get behind the legends to the facts. Yet, whatever level of understanding of the New Testament these men may have had (and it will be remembered that individual Christians rarely saw, never mind possessed, a copy of the Bible until after the invention of printing in the fifteenth century), these cell groups were composed of men with burdened hearts. In the early days of Celtic monasticism, their message and the manner of their lives had a powerful impact throughout the land.

In Ninian we find a man who is so obscure that the dates of his life have not been definitely established, yet the echoes of his ministry have sounded down through the years. We might well be reminded of the words of the great eighteenth-century evangelist George Whitefield (whose life is far better documented), "Let the name of Whitefield perish, but let the name of Christ endure." We should never forget that in actual fact most of the history of the Christian church remains unwritten, precisely because God delights to use the obscure.

Another lesson we learn from both Ninian and Columba is that the power of the gospel is best expressed in community life, no matter how small. The Apostle Paul was rarely alone. He did not travel around the ancient world as an individual but as the leader of a mobile gospel cell group. The gospel message and its manifestation in the life of the church go hand-in-glove in New Testament evangelism. How odd, then, if our churches persist in sending individual church planters instead of a cell group to begin a new work. We surely need to return to the New Testament pattern and to the genius of these monk-evangelists.

But the principle is more widely applicable than to church planting. There is a contemporary pattern of growing bigger churches. In turn, this means bigger buildings, often bigger financial loans, and the necessity to grow even bigger in order to finance the bigness of things. We need a different goal: to grow closer, deeper, more local, and more visible in the community, if the gospel is to make its true impact on our Western world.

In addition, we are in great need of heroic Christianity—young men and women delivered from what Christopher Lasch called "the cult of narcissism."[8] These missionary-monks were willing to go anywhere and do anything simply because Christ had called them. We need to be willing to do that, and to encourage our young people to be willing to do it too. Sometimes Christian parents speak of rearing their children "to be the next generation's leaders in our society." That is not a New Testament vision. Rather, we are called to nurture them to be servants—servants of Jesus Christ who are willing to be servants of others and therefore willing to reject the values of this society for those of the kingdom of Christ and the need of the world.

There are, indeed, lessons to be learned from the lives of Ninian and Columba. They are needed just as much in the twenty-first century as they were in the sixth.

Christ Is the World's Redeemer

ATTRIBUTED TO COLUMBA[9]

Christ is the world's Redeemer,
The lover of the pure,
The Fount of heavenly wisdom,
Our trust and hope secure;
The Armour of His soldiers,
The Lord of earth and sky;
Our Health while we are living,
Our Life when we shall die.

Christ hath our host surrounded
With clouds of martyrs bright,
Who wave their palms in triumph,
And fire us for the fight.
Christ the red cross ascended,
To save a world undone,
And, suffering for the sinful,
Our full redemption won.

All glory to the Father,
The unbegotten One;
All honor be to Jesus,
His sole begotten Son;
And to the Holy Spirit—
The perfect Trinity.
Let all the worlds give answer,
"Amen—so let it be."

Down in the realm of darkness
He lay a captive bound,
But at the hour appointed
He rose, a Victor crowned;

And now, to heaven ascended,
He sits upon the throne,
In glorious dominion,
His Father's, and his own.

7

THE SEVENTH CENTURY

GREGORY AND MUHAMMAD

The text below (quoted in Bede's Ecclesiastical History of the English People*) is from a pastoral letter from Pope Boniface VIII to Queen Ethelberga, the daughter of the first Christian king of Kent. He also wrote to her husband, Edwin, king of Northumbria, urging him to become a Christian. On Easter Day 627, Edwin professed Christian faith and was baptized along with their son, Ethelhun.*

To the illustrious lady his daughter, Queen Ethelberga, Boniface, bishop, servant of the servants of God: The goodness of our Redeemer has with much providence offered the means of salvation to the human race, which he rescued, by the shedding of his precious blood, from the bonds of captivity to the Devil; so that making his name known in divers ways to the Gentiles, they might acknowledge their Creator by embracing the mystery of the Christian faith, which thing, the mystical purification of your regeneration plainly shows to have been bestowed upon the mind of your highness by God's bounty. Our mind, therefore, has been much rejoiced in the benefit of our Lord's goodness, for that he has vouchsafed, in your conversion, to kindle a spark of the orthodox religion, by which he might the more easily inflame in his love the understanding, not only of your glorious consort, but also of all the nation that is subject to you.

For we have been informed by those, who came to acquaint us with the laudable conversion of our illustrious son, King Eadbald, that your highness, also, having received the wonderful sacrament of the Christian faith, continually excels in the performance of works pious and acceptable to God. That you likewise carefully refrain from the worship of idols, and the deceits of temples and auguries, and having changed your devotion, are so wholly taken up with the love of your Redeemer, as never to cease lending your assistance for the propagation of the Christian faith. And our fatherly charity having earnestly inquired concerning your illustrious husband, we were given to understand, that he still served abominable idols, and would not yield obedience or give ear to the voice of the preachers. This occasioned us no small grief, for that part of your body still remained a stranger to the knowledge of the supreme and undivided Trinity. Whereupon we, in our fatherly care, did not delay to admonish your Christian highness, exhorting you, that, with the help of the Divine inspiration, you will not defer to do that which, both in season and out of season, is required of us; that with the co-operating power of our Lord and Saviour Jesus Christ, your husband also may be added to the number of Christians; to the end that you may thereby enjoy the rights of marriage in the bond of a holy and unblemished union. For it is written, "The two shall be in one flesh." How can it be said, that there is unity between you, if he continues a stranger to the brightness of your faith, by the interposition of dark and detestable error?

Wherefore, applying yourself continually to prayer, do not cease to beg of the Divine Mercy the benefit of his illumination; to the end, that those whom the union of carnal affection has made in a manner but one body, may, after death, continue in perpetual union, by the bond of faith. Persist, therefore, illustrious daughter, and to the utmost of your power endeavour to soften the hardness of his heart by insinuating the Divine precepts; making him sensible how noble the mystery is which you have received by believing, and how wonderful is the reward which, by the new birth, you have merited to obtain. Inflame the coldness of his heart by the knowledge of the Holy Ghost, that by the abolition of the cold and pernicious worship of paganism, the heat of Divine faith may enlighten his understanding through your frequent exhortations; that the testimony of the holy Scripture may appear the more conspicuous, fulfilled by you, "The unbelieving husband shall be saved by the believing wife." For to this effect you have obtained the mercy of our Lord's goodness, that you may return with increase the fruit of faith, and the benefits entrusted in your hands; for through the assistance of His mercy we do not cease with frequent prayers to beg that you may be able to perform the same.

Having premised thus much, in pursuance of the duty of our fatherly affection, we exhort you, that when the opportunity of a bearer shall offer, you will as soon as possible acquaint us with the success which the Divine Power shall grant by your means in the conversion of your consort, and of the nation subject to you; to the end, that our solicitude, which earnestly expects what appertains to the salvation of you and yours, may, by hearing from you, be set at rest.

———

The seventh century stands as far removed from the events of the New Testament as we are from the events of the Protestant Reformation. Much had transpired in the intervening years, as we have seen. But this century was to see the emergence of two figures who would make lasting impacts on the story of the Christian church. The significance of one of them is obvious. The other is someone we might not immediately think of including in a survey of the *Christian* church. For he himself was not part of it.

Gregory

The first figure straddles the centuries and died as the seventh century was still in its opening years. He was Gregory (the Great), pope from 590 to 604. His influence dominated the church well into the rest of the century.

Gregory (540–604) was brought up in a wealthy, aristocratic Italian family. His father, Gordianus, was a senator. Having shown unusual giftedness in the study of the law, he was appointed prefect of Rome around 570. But soon afterward, he came to a critical decision to renounce the world and decided to become a monk. He sold his property and donated the considerable proceeds to the needs of the poor and to the establishment of monasteries. His outstanding abilities led to a rise through the ranks of the church hierarchy until he was eventually, albeit apparently reluctantly, elected pope.

Gregory possessed outstanding organizational ability, which was coupled with an ambitious vision for the church. He continued to be involved in civil government, wrote on the pastoral office of the bishop, and also did much to promote the monastic life. In short, he pursued the goal of strengthening the role of the papacy and thereby enhancing the effectiveness of the church.

Gregory held the view that Christ had made the bishops of Rome archbishops of the whole church. The pope was, therefore, Christ's own vicar, His representative on earth. In that role, the pope had the task of laying claim to the whole world for Christ, with all secular powers subject to him.

One of the ways in which this vision was furthered was through the sending of bands of monks and evangelists throughout the known world in order to baptize the people and to place the name of Christ over the nations. In that respect, Gregory was, at least superficially, enormously successful. Rulers and kings were won to the (now Roman) Catholic Church. Nations at large were baptized. It must have seemed, at least outwardly, that the "Vicar of Christ" was bringing in the reign of his Master not only spiritually but visibly.

Creating "Christian" nations in this way, however, is bound—to use Paul's language—to produce the form of godliness without its power (see 2 Tim. 3:5), the name but not the reality. This is always the kind of nominal Christianity produced by a misfocused view that the world can be won to Christ by the act of baptism without a community that clearly understands the gospel and has been changed by it. The Christian church has been struggling with the consequences ever since.

It is perhaps not surprising, then, that Gregory would also encourage a number of other elements in the faith and practice of the church which would lead it further from "the simplicity that is in Christ" (2 Cor. 11:3, KJV). These included an emphatic development of the view (earlier entertained by Augustine) of the need for purification after death, which would later be hardened into the doctrine of purgatory. Gregory further confused the free grace of God in the work of Christ by developing the notion of penance as satisfaction for the temporal guilt of sin. In addition, he contributed to the notion of the Mass as a sacrifice in which Christ is the victim. It is perhaps not surprising that he viewed individual assurance of faith as not a desirable thing for the ordinary Christian.

Thus, it is striking that it was precisely as the church was becoming strong as a political force, but growing weak in its hold on the gospel, that another figure staked his claim to be a major figure in history. His name was Abū al-Qāsim Muḥammad ibn ʿAbd Allāh ibn ʿAbd al-Muṭṭalib ibn Hāshim. We know him simply as Muhammad.

Muhammad

Born around 570, Muhammad was orphaned as a child. He seems to have suffered from various illnesses, including possibly a form of epilepsy.

He was untutored, uneducated, and possibly even illiterate. At the age of twenty-five, he married a widow some fifteen years older and became a trader. His wife bore him six children, with only his daughter Fatima surviving into adulthood. Through his work, he met Jews and Christians and began to listen to what they believed. But he gained only a very inadequate understanding of the gospel.

During his middle years, Muhammad claimed to have experienced supernatural visions. In the first of these, he said the archangel Gabriel called him to be the prophet of God. He began to preach and teach the Five Pillars of Islam: (1) *Shahadah*: the confession that there is no God but Allah, and Muhammad is his prophet; (2) *Salat*: the duty of ritual prayer five times a day; (3) *Zakāt*: the necessity of engaging in acts of charity; (4) *Sawm*: fasting during the month of Ramadan; and (5) *Hajj*: the great pilgrimage to Mecca.

At first, he found very little response apart from his own family; beyond them he found only hostility. People questioned his stability.

In the year 622, Muhammad fled to Medina (then known as Yathrib, in western Saudi Arabia). This event—known as the *Hijra*—marks the beginning of the Islamic calendar. In Medina, he began to gather large numbers of followers. In 629, he returned to Mecca with an army of ten thousand and took the city in a virtually bloodless conquest. By the time of his death in 632, he had gathered around forty thousand to fifty thousand adherents to his teachings. In various places, these followers began to molest and indeed virtually destroy tribes of Jews and Christians. Islam as a religion had begun.

By the beginning of the eighth century, within only eighty years of Muhammad's original vision, the entire Roman Empire was overrun. With extraordinary rapidity, Islam spread through North Africa and into southern Europe, both west and east, over a region of some four to five thousand miles. As the Islamic *jihad* (holy war, or struggle) continued, pagans were required to accept Islam or death. "People of the Book" (i.e., Jews and Christians) were given a third choice of *jizyah*, a per capita tax. This was justified on the grounds that they would not be involved in military activity and therefore were required to pay a levy as a substitute.

The name *Islam*, meaning "surrender" or "submission," and the character of its activity underline what lies at the very heart of the religion—belief in one god, whom the Qur'an describes as one "to whom one may appeal for mercy," but in relationship to whom the essential issue is a total and, it appears, fatalistic submission. Hence the often-used expression "If Allah wills it."

Muhammad rejected cardinal elements of the Christian faith. In particular, he reduced Christ to the level of other prophets. He denied that Jesus actually died on the cross—a substitute had taken His place, it was claimed.[1] Clearly, then, Muhammad's Christ was neither the Christ of the New Testament nor was He One who could provide salvation.

Islam called for submission to the will of Allah and offered the prospects of heavenly rewards for righteousness. There is nothing here of the pardoning, restoring, transforming grace of God in Jesus Christ, nothing of a great transaction between Christ and the heavenly Father in which Christ bore our sins and offers the assurance of salvation. In other words, Islam belongs to the category of world religions that lack both a God of infinite holiness and infinite love and the hope of salvation for deeply sinful man.

Why should the origins of Islam feature in a book like this? Because a knowledge of this history has much to teach us in the present time.

Much later, we will encounter a major transformation in the underlying thinking of the Western world. Put simply, the new assumption is this: since we cannot have certain knowledge of God (if He exists at all), all we are left with is that all religions are descriptions of religious experience. Ultimately, they all are doing the same thing, some better than others. But more than that we cannot say. Thus, in our modern world, Christianity and Islam are seen as two different forms of the same basic religion, two expressions of man's "spiritual side."

For this reason, people often make the mistake of thinking that it makes little difference to society which one is preferred—so long as we maintain respect for our shared traditions and cause no harm. After all, underneath all religion, it is assumed, is the fact that human beings—granted, there have been a few notorious exceptions—are basically good.

So long as no religion is given priority, we can essentially return to the happy condition we enjoyed before "fundamentalist" Christianity made its exclusivist claims.

There is both a deep naïvete and an ignorance of history in this perspective. It is indeed a remarkable illustration of Hegel's lament.

The truth is that the Western world was pagan before the coming of the gospel. What has long been seen as "civilized" behavior is a *fruit* of the gospel, not its *forerunner*. And to regard Christianity and Islam as essentially the same is simply another expression of the contemporary mantra: "Don't all roads lead to God?" But this question fails to grapple with another more important one: "On what basis can we stand in His presence when we get there?" Islam is a way of submission and good works. There is no good news there. By contrast, the gospel is a message of God's grace, of faith and hope and love—a message about God's seeking us and finding us. Nor should we lose sight of the stubborn fact that until the days of Constantine, the remarkable spread of Christianity took place exclusively by the preaching of the gospel and never by military activity. We are dealing here not with two variants but two antithetical views of God.

Before we leave this momentous century, it is sobering to remember what the church was doing when Islam was on the march.

Part of the answer to that question makes for discouraging reading. In 663–64, a now-famous gathering of churchmen took place in Whitby in Yorkshire in the northeast of England. At precisely the time Islam was advancing—a force in some senses far more destructive to the church than the Roman Empire had ever been—what were the topics that required serious discussion? The synod had been called because Oswy, king of Northumbria, realized that the following year when he was observing Easter (according to the Celtic calendar that had been used in the churches of Columba), his wife (who was reared under the Roman Catholic calendar) would still be observing Lent. A crisis indeed.

The Synod of Whitby came to be known for two decisions: (1) the shape of the tonsure worn by priests and monks, and (2) the date when Easter should be celebrated. There is, of course, a place for discussing church calendars; even a discussion of hairstyles may have its place (see Rom. 14:5–6; 1 Cor. 11:6, 14–16). But for tonsures and calendars to be the major items debated at such a time as this was surely shortsighted in setting the church's priorities.

How tragic, when the great question is, How can we obey the Great Commission to bring the gospel to the ends of the earth?

Will we ever learn from history?

A Great and Mighty Wonder

GERMANUS, PATRIARCH OF CONSTANTINOPLE (634–734)[2]

A great and mighty wonder.
A full and holy cure:
The Virgin bears the Infant
With virgin honor pure.
Repeat the hymn again:
"To God on high be glory
And peace on earth to men!"

The Word becomes incarnate
And yet remains on high,
And cherubim sing anthems
To shepherds from the sky.
Repeat the hymn again:
"To God on high be glory
And peace on earth to men!"

While thus they sing your Monarch,
Those bright angelic bands,
Rejoice, ye vales and mountains,
Ye oceans, clap your hands.
Repeat the hymn again:
"To God on high be glory
And peace on earth to men!"

Since all He comes to ransom.
By all be He adored,
The Infant born in Bethl'em,
The Saviour and the Lord.
Repeat the hymn again:
"To God on high be glory
And peace on earth to men!"

And idol forms shall perish,
And error shall decay,
And Christ shall wield His sceptre,
Our Lord and God for aye.
Repeat the hymn again:
"To God on high be glory
And peace on earth to men!"

8

THE EIGHTH CENTURY

DISPUTES OVER IMAGES

The Sigan-Fu Stone is a door-size stone slab discovered in northwest China by Roman Catholic missionaries in 1623 or 1625. Set up in 781, it records events regarding the Christian church of the previous 150 years from the time when a missionary monk, known to the Chinese as A-lo-pen, had come from Syria to China to bring the good news of the gospel. The slab is more than nine feet (2.79 m) high, is made of black limestone, and is today preserved in the Forest of Stelae in Xian. Its text is excerpted below.

. . . the illustrious and honourable Messiah, veiling his true dignity, appeared in the world as a man; angelic powers promulgated the glad tidings, a virgin gave birth to the Holy One in Syria; a bright star announced the felicitous event, and Persians observing the splendour came to present tribute; the ancient dispensation, as declared by the twenty-four holy men [the writers of the Old Testament], was then fulfilled, and he laid down great principles for the government of families and kingdoms; he established the new religion of the silent operation of the pure spirit of the Triune; he rendered virtue subservient to direct faith; he fixed the extent of the eight boundaries, thus completing the truth and freeing it from dross; he opened the gate of the three constant principles, introducing life and destroying death; he suspended the bright sun to invade the chambers of darkness, and the falsehoods of the devil were thereupon defeated; he set in motion the vessel of mercy by which to ascend to the bright mansions, whereupon rational beings were then released, having thus completed the manifestation of his power, in clear day he ascended to his true station. Twenty-seven sacred books [the number in the New Testament] have been left, which disseminate intelligence by unfolding the original trans-forming principles. By the rule for admission, it is the custom to apply the water of baptism, to wash away all superficial show and to cleanse and purify the neophytes. As a seal, they hold the cross, whose influence is reflected in every direction, uniting all without distinction. As they strike the wood, the fame of their benevolence is diffused abroad; worshiping toward the east, they hasten on the way to life and glory; they preserve the beard to symbolize their outward actions, they shave the crown to indicate the absence of inward affections; they do not keep slaves, but put noble and mean all on an equality; they do not amass wealth, but cast all their prop-erty into the common stock; they fast, in order to perfect themselves by self-inspection; they submit to restraints, in order to strengthen themselves by silent watchfulness; seven times a day they have wor-ship and praise for the benefit of the living and the dead; once in seven days they sacrifice, to cleanse the heart and return to purity. It is difficult to find a name to express the excellence of the true and unchangeable doctrine; but as its meritorious operations are manifestly displayed, by accommodation it is named the Illustri-ous Religion. Now without holy men, principles cannot become expanded; without principles, holy men cannot become magnified; but with holy men and right principles, united as the two parts of a signet, the world becomes civilized and enlightened. In the time of the accomplished Emperor Tai-tsung, the illustrious and mag-nificent founder of the dynasty, among the enlightened and holy men who arrived was the most-virtuous Olopun, from the coun-try of Syria. Observing the azure clouds, he bore the true sacred books; beholding the direction of the winds, he braved difficulties and dangers. In the year of our Lord 635, he arrived at Chang-an; the Emperor sent his Prime Minister, Duke Fang Hiuen-ling; who, carrying the official staff to the west border, conducted his guest into the interior; the sacred books were translated in the imperial library, the sovereign investigated the subject in his private apartments; when becoming deeply impressed with the rectitude and truth of the religion, he gave special orders for its dissemination.

———

We are used to reading books about the Christian faith written in English. We often forget that English is not the language in which most of church history has been lived out.

Many Christian churches of the first millennium increasingly expressed themselves in theology and worship in two languages: Latin and Greek. Latin was the *lingua franca* of the church in the West, centered in Rome; Greek dominated in the Eastern church, centered in Constantinople.

Two Polarities

Undoubtedly, this regional linguistic split had effects. For one thing, it meant that two different theological vocabularies came into being. Thus, when the church in the West confessed that God is Trinity, it spoke of Him as three persons (*personae*) in one substance (*substantia*). But in the East, the term used for each person was *hupostasis*. God is three persons (*hupostaseis*) in one being or substance (*ousia*). The problem? *Substantia* and *hupostasis* are equivalent in structure but were used to denote different elements in the definition. To the Greek ear, the Latin might appear to be an expression of modalism; to the Latin ear, the Greek might sound like an expression of tritheism.

While this early complexity was ironed out, it was indicative that the two communities were developing different ways of speaking and thinking about the gospel. The geographic distance between Rome and Constantinople, the two "centers of authority," and their corresponding independent leadership did not help. One aspect of the difference in traditions came to a head in the eighth century over the question of the nature and use of icons in the worship of God.

An Iconic Controversy

An icon (from the Greek *eikōn*, "image") is usually an oil painting on wood of our Lord Jesus, frequently of the Virgin Mary, or sometimes of a saint. Although in earlier centuries paintings and statues had been prohibited in the churches, from around the fifth century onward, icons had become especially popular in the Eastern church.

The church's argument for having them was straightforward enough:

most believers were simple and uneducated people; they neither possessed Bibles of their own, nor could they read, but through pictures, they could be helped to understand the message of the gospel.

The attendant danger is obvious. When an object (or a person, for that matter) becomes closely associated with the divine, the time may come when the reverence due to the divine is shared by or even transferred to that object (or person). That can happen as easily with a communion table ("the holy table"), or even with a favorite preacher, as it did with icons. Thus, the icons were kissed, and in some (theoretically lesser) sense the reverence directed toward the person they symbolized (divine or human) was transferred to the icon itself. Icons began to be viewed as channels through which Christ brought blessing to His people. On occasion, incense (a worship symbol) would be burned before them as an expression of desire that through the figure pictured on the icon the Heavenly Father would hear the prayers of His people.

For many, the use of icons constituted a breach of the commandment forbidding bowing down before and worshiping images (see Ex. 20:4–5). It was, therefore, a major additional hindrance to the evangelization of both Jews and Muslims.

The controversy was extended and at times became vicious. Monks who had vigorously defended icons were persecuted. On the other hand, the greatest theologian of the Eastern church, John of Damascus (c. 655–750), wrote in their defense. A synod called by Constantine V at Hiera in 753 required the destruction of icons, but its decision was reversed at Nicaea in 787. The controversy continued throughout the rest of the century and into the first half of the next, when the Eastern church officially approved the use of icons. The underlying tensions between East and West would come to a climax two hundred years later in the Great Schism, which created a division that continues to the present day.

Two major issues were highlighted by this ancient controversy.

It would be a very superficial reading of the Iconoclastic Controversy to think of it as merely a debate over whether the church is for or against works of art. The Western Christian tradition abounds in works of art. Indeed, it would even be a mistake to think that the Western church separated art from the church—after all, every new church building project raises questions about how the gospel relates to architecturally expressed art.

The deeper issue was, in one sense, about God's commandments, and particularly the forbidding of images' being reverenced and adored. Once we turn a man-made object into an article to be reverenced, ordinarily it will not be long before our worship becomes superstitious. In another sense, the debate was over sacraments—does God "communicate" Himself and His grace through icons? Admiration of art, stimulation of love for God, reminders of His person and work—all of these can take place in a wide variety of contexts and through many different means. But are they God-ordained means to worship Him, and do they constitute the "sacraments" through which He communicates His love to us?[1]

The New Testament church was also constituted, largely, of ordinary people. But its worship was simple. It did indeed have "icons." For Jesus had given the whole church two of them.

The first is the icon of baptism, the symbol that points us to the washing away of our sins through union with Christ. The second is the Lord's Supper—the taking of bread and wine that makes real to us the words of Jesus: "Behold, I stand at the door and knock. If anyone hears my voice and opens the door, I will come in to him and eat with him, and he with me" (Rev. 3:20, KJV).

But before we leave the Iconoclastic Controversy, it is worth asking if Protestants have been iconoclastic in the wrong sense—failing our Lord by a disregard of the two icons He has given to us. Twenty-first-century Christians do not seem to give their baptism much thought after the event itself, unless to debate it. And then, imagine members of a congregation being given a blank card after the Lord's Supper and asked to fill in what—if anything—they think "happened" at the service. Could we be confident that the answers in our own church family would display simplicity, clarity, unity—and even orthodoxy? So, perhaps if we are critical of the use of icons in the Eastern church, we ought also to be critical of ourselves that we have paid so little attention to the "icons" we believe Jesus has given to us.

Mystery Plays

In addition, at its best, the issue of icons raises a legitimate and indeed important concern. If people do not, will not, or cannot read the Scriptures, how do we communicate the gospel to them?

This was the argument that lay behind the justification of the so-called mystery plays—portrayals of biblical stories or the lives of saints—in the Middle Ages. In a sense, it was the same concern that birthed the early Puritan William Perkins' burden to produce his "ocular catechism" in his Golden Chain of Salvation—a visual, diagrammatic representation of the way of salvation. John Bunyan shared the same burden and later produced his own version of it. Indeed, with great genius, he expressed the gospel in the form of an allegorical drama in *The Pilgrim's Progress*. So, there is an issue latent within the Iconoclastic Controversy that every generation of Christians must face if we are to discharge our responsibility to communicate the gospel. How do we do this to people who are ignorant of it? The most obviously recurring error in this context is to do it without constantly anchoring our thinking and methods in the teaching and patterns of the Scriptures and analyzing and addressing our culture in the light of God's Word.

Sadly, in the eighth century, the controversy turned the church inward. Meanwhile, the world outside was perishing for lack of the knowledge of Jesus Christ.

Thankfully, in the eighth century, we also find a focus on more central things. This can be illustrated in two very different ways.

Boniface (672–754)

Around the year 672 in the area of Wessex, England,[2] a child by the name of Wynfrith (sometimes written "Wynfrid") was born. He is known to history as Boniface. A young man of considerable intellectual gifts, he committed himself to the monastic way of life and became an itinerant evangelist in various places, including Frisia, Thuringia, and Bavaria.

His first evangelistic tour to Frisia in 716 was a failure. Undaunted, he pressed on under a commission from Gregory II (pope from 715 to 731).

Boniface is best remembered for one particular action. In the area of Geismar in Hesse stood a great tree known as "the Oak of Thor."[3] It was regarded as a sacred object. As a sign of his confidence in Christ and the gospel, Boniface, Elijah-like, challenged his pagan opponents and personally hacked down the great tree. It was a wonderful illustration of his courage but also of his sense that the whole earth is the Lord's; those who trust and obey are safe until their life's work is completed. In a sense, Boniface was simply saying, "All authority here in Geismar belongs to the Lord Jesus Christ; that is why I have come to proclaim and demonstrate that His kingdom has come!" Boniface himself was martyred for Christ in 754.

Even the Stones Cry Out[4]

Another little-known event from the eighth century speaks volumes about the hidden spread of the gospel: the Sigan-Fu Stone. This slab (the size of a massive door[5]) was discovered in the early seventeenth century by Roman Catholic missionaries in China who believed that they were moving into virgin territory for the church. It had been set up in 781 and recorded the events of the Christian church of the previous 150 years from the time when a missionary monk, known to the Chinese as A-lo-pen, had come from Syria to China to bring the good news of the gospel. By the next century, just at the time the stone was being inscribed by perhaps one of the last living Christians in China, the emperors had sought to completely suppress all testimony to Jesus Christ and worship of His name.

What would A-lo-pen have thought of the vast number of Christians in China today? He was truly a grain of wheat that fell to the ground to die that has not remained alone but has borne much fruit.

Boniface and A-lo-pen—two eighth-century missionaries of the cross. Some Christians today may be tempted to focus on their theological shortcomings, especially Boniface's devotion to the pope as his spiritual leader. Doubtless, as Christians of their time, they had their inconsistencies. But how inconsistent of us if we sit in judgment on what we regard as their failures, yet also sit in silence and comfort rather than speak the gospel and go to the ends of the earth to tell others about Christ as they did. These men illustrate two of the characteristics Christ looks for in contemporary Christians: to stand for Christ in a pagan environment—whatever it costs—like Boniface, and the willingness to go wherever God sends us, like A-lo-pen.

Some self-examination is surely in order. Am I, perhaps, the kind of Christian who is quick to be caught up in a controversy (which may indeed have its place) while ignoring the call to world evangelism? Then let me remember Boniface, the Sigan-Fu Stone, and most of all, let me remember Jesus Christ crucified and risen from the dead that He might be my Lord.

The Day of Resurrection! Earth, Tell It Out Abroad

JOHN OF DAMASCUS (675–749)[6]

The day of resurrection! Earth, tell it out abroad;
The Passover of gladness, the Passover of God.
From death to life eternal, from earth unto the sky,
Our Christ hath brought us over, with hymns of victory.

Our hearts be pure from evil, that we may see aright
The Lord in rays eternal of resurrection light;
And listening to His accents, may hear, so calm and plain,
His own "All hail!" and, hearing, may raise the victor strain.

Now let the heavens be joyful! Let earth the song begin!
Let the round world keep triumph, and all that is therein!
Let all things seen and unseen their notes in gladness blend,
For Christ the Lord hath risen, our joy that hath no end.

9

THE NINTH CENTURY

CONFLICT AND SACRIFICE

Gottschalk was a deeply controversial figure because of his Augustinian views of God's grace and sovereignty in salvation. His **Shorter Confession concerning Double Predestination** *follows.*

I believe and confess that *the* omnipotent and unchangeable God foreknew and predestined *holy* ahngels and elect men to eternal life gratis and that He equally predestined *the* devil, head of all demons, with all of his apostates, and also reprobate men, namely his members, on account of their own most certainly foreknown evil merits, through the most right judgment to deserved eternal death; for thus says the Lord Himself in His Gospel: "The prince of this world is already judged." What blessed Augustine explained for people is therefore publicly expressed so: "That is irrevocably destined to eternal fire." Likewise the Truth itself about the reprobate: "Whoever does not believe is judged already," that is to say is already damned. He says: "The judgment has not yet appeared, but already it has taken place." Likewise, commenting on these words of John the Baptist: "His testimony is not accepted by anybody," he says thus: "By anybody that is by a certain people, which is prepared for the wrath of God, to be damned with the devil." Likewise about Jews: "They were angry, those dead and predestined to eternal death." Likewise: "Why did the Lord say to Jews: 'You do not believe, because you are no sheep of mine,' unless He saw them predestined to everlasting destruction, not won to eternal life by the price of His own blood?" Likewise commenting on these words of the Lord: "The sheep that belong to Me listen to My voice; I know them and they follow Me. I give them eternal life; they will never be lost and no one will ever steal them from My hand. The Father, for what He has given Me, is greater than anyone, and no one can steal anything from the Father's hand," he said so: "What can the wolf do? What can the thief and the robber? They destroy none but those predestined to destruction." Likewise speaking about two worlds: "The whole world is the Church, and yet the whole world hates the Church. The world therefore hates the world, the hostile that which is reconciled, the condemned that which is saved, the polluted that which is cleansed." Likewise: "For there is a world about which the apostle says: 'That we might not be condemned with this world.' For that world the Lord does not pray, for He does not ignore to what it is predestined." Likewise: "Judas, the betrayer of Christ, was called the son of perdition, predestined to perdition." Likewise in *Enchiridion*: "To the damnation of those whom He justly predestined to punishment." Likewise in his book *On the Perfection of Human Righteousness* he says: "This good, which is required, nobody has done, not a single person. But so in that race of men, which is predestined for perdition. For God's foreknowledge took notice of them and pronounced the sentence on them." Likewise in his book *On the City of God*: "Who has given such things even to those whom He has predestined to death." Likewise blessed pope Gregory: "This Leviathan with all of his members is deputed to eternal tortures." Likewise Saint Fulgentius in the third book *On the Truth of Predestination and Grace* says: "God certainly prepared punishment for those sinners whom He justly predestined to suffer torments." Blessed Fulgentius composed a whole book concerning this particular question, that is, on the predestination of the reprobate to destruction, for his friend named Monimus. On which basis also Saint Isidore says: "Predestination is twofold: either of the elect to rest or of the reprobate to death." Therefore so I believe and confess everything with these elect of God and catholic men, inasmuch as I am divinely inspired, animated, equipped. Amen.

———

Word association experiments can be fascinating. Often the mention of a word immediately brings its opposite to mind: good/bad, short/tall, wise/foolish.

East . . . West?

In the early centuries of the Christian church, these polarities were not only geographical; they were historical, cultural, linguistic, and also *theological.* Tensions inevitably grew.

These points of tension involved not only the use of icons but a vigorous disagreement over what is known as the *filioque* clause. This concerned the relationship of the Holy Spirit to the other two persons of the Godhead.

The Apostles' Creed had simply stated, "I believe . . . in the Holy Spirit. . . ."

As late as the Nicene Creed (formulated at the first ecumenical council of 325), this same simplicity prevailed: "We believe . . . in the Holy Spirit. . . ." The second ecumenical council held at Constantinople in 381 developed this into a series of beautiful statements that in the version used in the East read:

I believe . . .
In the Holy Spirit, the Lord and Giver of life,
Who proceeds from the Father,
Who together with the Father and the Son is worshiped
    and glorified,
Who has spoken through the prophets. . . .

In the West, however, the words "who proceeds from the Father" became "who proceeds from the Father *and from the Son* (Latin *filioque*). Especially under the influence of Augustine's teaching on the Trinity, which emphasized the mutual relations of all three persons, this became the orthodoxy of the Latin church, which now confessed:

Credo . . .
Et in Spiritum Sanctum, Dominum et vivificantem,
qui ex Patre Filioque *procedit. . . .*

We will meet up with one of the major consequences of this addition when we come to the eleventh century. But for the moment, it is worthwhile to pause and reflect on a perennial challenge to the church when it engages in internal doctrinal disputes.

Doctrinal Conflict

Scripture is God-breathed (2 Tim. 3:16), its authors superintended by the Holy Spirit in order to reveal the mind of God. But whenever there is theology, there is always psychology. To put it more pointedly, theologians never engage in controversy as depersonalized, purified brains but as sinful people. All too often, mixed into the discussions are the personalities and agendas of the participants, and, alas, often a distasteful and sinful love of self, position, and power. So, while there were genuine theological concerns about the *filioque* clause, it also developed within the context of an ecclesiastical power struggle between East and West.

The seeds of this struggle had already been sown in the ninth century and came to a head in the two figureheads of the respective churches: Nicholas I, pope in the Western church (858–67), a man of great organizational skills and a theologian and preacher, and in the Eastern church, Photius (810–95), the patriarch of Constantinople.

In the controversy, Nicholas appealed to what are now known as "the Pseudo-Isidorean Decretals."[1]

Isidore of Seville (c. 560–636) was a Spanish bishop and an influential church leader and theologian (among other things, he gave major support to the *filioque* clause). It was claimed he was the Isidore Mercator (or at least closely connected to him) who published a collection of documents including the so-called *Donatio Constantini*, or Donation of Constantine. This was a document under the name of the emperor Constantine that granted the pope authority over all the churches, specifically including Constantinople (which in the ninth century was the epicenter of the Eastern church, with Photius as its patriarch). It also granted the pope the power to overrule councils of the church. This was virtually ultimate power.

In 863, Nicholas deposed Photius from the patriarchate of Constantinople. Four years later at a council in Constantinople, Photius returned the favor and deposed, excommunicated, and anathematized the pope (all the while giving his reasons for rejecting the *filioque* clause).

Were it not for the forewarnings and counsel God has given us in Scripture, we might well despair of the church and its long catalog of power struggles. But reading the story of these two church leaders, we are surely reminded of the words of the Apostle John: "Diotrephes, who likes to put himself first, does not acknowledge our [Apostolic] authority . . . he refuses to welcome the brothers, and also stops those who want to and puts them out of the church" (3 John 9–10).

There are few things more destructive to the Christian church as a whole or to any congregation, large or small, than an individual who "loveth to have the preeminence" (3 John 9, KJV). And yet, as we have seen before, God never leaves Himself without a testimony to the saving and transforming power of the gospel.

A (Very Small) Band of Brothers

Two of the most remarkable Christians of the ninth century came from Thessalonica, the city first evangelized by the Apostle Paul in a memorable visit that lasted only a matter of weeks (Acts 17:1–10). Once again, "the word of the Lord sounded forth" from that ancient city (1 Thess. 1:8) in the person of two brothers, Cyril (826–69) and Methodius (815–85), who became evangelists to the Slavic peoples.

Most of us have heard of the Cyrillic alphabet used in many Slavic languages, even if we have only a vague idea of what it is. Its importance can be measured by the fact that it is used by about the same number of people as there are native English speakers in the United States. It is called "Cyrillic" after the younger of these two ninth-century missionary monks.

Cyril and Methodius evangelized the entire region around the Black Sea. The Christian churches there can trace their origins back to these brothers' mission. Even before Cyril and Methodius began their enterprise, they engaged in disciplined learning of the languages of the local peoples, creating an alphabet that could be used in Bible translation, thus bringing the gospel to this region in permanent form.

Here, then, are two brothers who well illustrate the important biblical and Christlike principle that seeds that are willing to fall into the ground and die bear much fruit (John 12:24).

In sharp contrast, a new view of the Christian life has taken hold of the contemporary imagination and, alas, has spread from the West to the East, as well as to the North and the South: the idea that the Christian life is one of happiness and not necessarily one of holiness, so that the "health, wealth, and happiness" gospel has spread throughout the world, infecting the air that Christians breathe. "Sacrifice"—a word that was dominant in earlier views of the Christian life—has virtually disappeared from the vocabulary. We have largely lost the sense that a life lived sacrificially for Christ, in obscurity, among those who have little, in places where there is no private medicine, few domestic comforts, low literacy rates, but a desperate need for the gospel and the teaching and training of Christians, can be a life whose fruit for eternity can be amazingly multiplied. Such were the brothers Cyril and Methodius. Their modern counterparts are, like them, living in obscurity. But are they a diminishing number?

God's Servant

Meanwhile, what was happening in the Western church? Important theological debates, especially about salvation. The story of one man who was engaged in these controversies has the potential to give us goose bumps. His name was Gottschalk—literally, "God's servant."

Gottschalk (804–69) was born in Saxony in the northern part of Germany. He was dedicated to the monastic life of the Benedictine Order as a boy—a decision that deeply troubled him in later life. In his mid-twenties, he transferred from the monastery at Fulda to Orbais. But in between, he spent time at the monastery of Corbie in Picardy. Remarkably, therefore, three of the most controversial figures in early ninth-century theology were simultaneously present at Corbie: along with Gottschalk, there were Paschasius Radbertus and Ratramnus, who engaged in fierce controversy over the question of the presence of Christ in the Lord's Supper.

Gottschalk's life was both marked and marred by controversy. As a monk, he was required to remain in his monastery. But sometime in the late 830s, he was ordained as a priest and became a missionary. He traveled to Italy and then to the Balkans.

But none of these details quite explains why Gottschalk proved to be such a controversial figure. The reason for that was the extent to which he had been drawn to the writings of Augustine, especially in his views on sin and grace.

Augustine had been captivated by the biblical teaching that we are not merely spiritually sick and in need of medicine. We are "dead in our trespasses" (Eph. 2:5). If we are to come to faith, and receive salvation, it can happen only and entirely by God's grace. It is not a matter of cooperation between God and man, each making his (or her) appropriate contribution. If I am *dead* in my sins, then I am incapable of contributing anything to my salvation.

As Gottschalk thought about this, he realized that Augustine was right to teach that if a person comes to faith in Christ, it must be because of God's initiative, not man's. God pursued us before we ever sought Him. This was indeed what the Apostle Paul had taught: if we come to faith, it is because we have been chosen in Christ "before the foundation of the world" (Eph. 1:4). But the young monk also saw that we cannot divide the sovereignty of God so that He predestines some events and simply lets others "happen." God's plan is not made up of occasional eternal forethoughts coupled with spontaneous historical interventions. It is a single, coherent whole. God decrees whatever comes to pass and "works all things according to the counsel of his will" (Eph. 1:11).

Gottschalk gathered a following of those who found his views to be biblical. He was not what we might think of as a professional theologian. He was a missionary and a preacher. Perhaps his views were not always well articulated or understood. He may not always have been the wisest of Christians (among other things, he seems to have been unusually averse to cleanliness!). But the defense of specific biblical doctrines that are under attack does not easily lend itself to comprehensive statement, nuanced expression, and balance. But this notwithstanding, Gottschalk's extant writings indicate that the substance of his teaching was similar to that of the Westminster Confession of Faith:

> By the decree of God, for the manifestation of His glory, some men and angels are predestined unto everlasting life; and others foreordained to everlasting death. . . .
>
> As God hath appointed the elect unto his own glory, so hath He, by the eternal and free purpose of His will, foreordained all the means thereunto. . . .
>
> The rest of mankind God was pleased, according to the unsearchable counsel of His own will, whereby he extendeth or withholdeth mercy, as He pleaseth, for the glory of His sovereign power over His creatures, to pass by; and to ordain them to dishonor and wrath for their sin, to the praise of His glorious justice. (WCF 3.3, 6, 7)

Various elements in this teaching provoked (and still provoke) sharp negative reactions. One was that the doctrine of predestination seemed to weaken the role of the organized church as mediator of salvation. Another was that it left no room for man's contribution to salvation (and thus effectively dismantled the growing semi-Pelagianism of the church). In addition, the idea that God had predestined the ultimate end of the lost was for many people a disturbing and distressing thought.

These emphases stun the mind and reverse all man-centered thinking. Their implications run both deep and wide. And when their impact is felt, they can easily overwhelm other considerations, including biblical ones. In addition, when a person grasps them but finds himself or herself in a church context where there is a deep prejudice against them, it becomes hard to speak of them without causing controversy. Gottschalk found himself in precisely this situation. At times, he may have been his own worst enemy. While he stressed that condemnation is based not on a divine whim but involves the just condemnation of those who are in themselves sinners, he may have become so "boxed in" by ecclesiastical opposition that he failed to strike the note later struck by the Westminster divines:

> The doctrine of this high mystery of predestination is to be *handled with special prudence and care, that men,* attending the will of God revealed in His Word, and yielding obedience thereunto, *may, from the certainty of their effectual vocation, be assured of their eternal election. So shall this doctrine afford matter of praise, reverence, and admiration of God; and of humility, diligence and abundant consolation, to all that sincerely obey the gospel.* (WCF 3.8, emphasis added)

Gottschalk was, however, given little opportunity to express that pastoral spirit. His appeals to the teaching of Augustine[2] (and other noteworthy figures in the church such as Isidore of Seville) were treated with arrogant contempt. Yet even from the perspective of anti-Augustinianism, he did not merit the treatment he received: branded a heretic, he was forced to throw his books into the fire, publicly flogged, deprived of his priesthood, and effectively imprisoned and condemned to perpetual silence.

When we make all possible allowances for the fact that Gottschalk's teaching might have been better expressed—even if he was the kind of believer whose personality probably makes them easier to live with in heaven when they are finally sanctified than on earth where they are imperfectly so—the treatment he received constituted a deep-seated hostility to biblical teaching on sin and grace.

Gottschalk stood courageously for the absolute necessity of God's sovereign grace in our salvation. Such men deserve to be honored, especially when in life they have been so severely dishonored. He died in 868. Now, 1,250 years later, he receives more honor than any of those who so cruelly demeaned him.

Jesus, Name All Names Above

THEOCTISTUS OF THE STUDIUM (DIED C. 890)[3]

Jesus, Name all names above,
Jesus, best and dearest;
Jesus, Fount of perfect love,
holiest, tenderest, nearest:
Jesus, Source of grace completest;
Jesus purest, Jesus sweetest;
Jesus, Well of power divine,
make me, keep me, seal me thine!

Woe that I have turned aside
after fleshly pleasure!
Woe that I have never tried
for the heavenly treasure!
Treasure, safe in homes supernal,
incorruptible, and eternal;
treasure no less price hath won
than the passion of the Son!

Jesus, crowned with thorns for me,
scourged for my transgression!
Witnessing, through agony,
that thy good confession!
Jesus, clad in purple raiment,
for my evils making payment:
let not all thy woe and pain,
let not Calvary be in vain!

Jesus, open me the gate
that of old he entered
who, in that most low estate,
wholly on thee ventured;

thou, whose wounds are ever pleading
and thy passion interceding,
from my misery let me rise
to a home in paradise!

10

___

THE TENTH CENTURY

A DARK TIME

The text below, on the state of the leadership of the visible church in the tenth century, is from a speech by Arnulf, bishop of Orleans, at the Synod of Verzy in 991.

Looking at the actual state of the papacy, what do we behold? John [XII] called Octavian, wallowing in the sty of filthy concupiscence, conspiring against the sovereign whom he had himself recently crowned; then Leo [VIII] the neophyte, chased from the city by this Octavian; and that monster himself, after the commission of many murders and cruelties, dying by the hand of an assassin. Next we see the deacon Benedict, though freely elected by the Romans, carried away captive into the wilds of Germany by the new Caesar [Otho I] and his pope Leo. Then a second Caesar [Otho II], greater in arts and arms than the first, succeeds; and in his absence Boniface, a very monster of iniquity, reeking with the blood of his predecessor, mounts the throne of Peter. True, he is expelled and condemned; but only to return again, and redden his hands with the blood of the holy bishop John [XIV].

Are there, indeed, any bold enough to maintain that the priests of the Lord over all the world are to take their law from monsters of guilt like these men branded with ignominy, illiterate men, and ignorant alike of things human and divine? If, holy, fathers, we be bound to weigh in the balance the lives, the morals, and the attainments of the meanest candidate for the sacerdotal office, how much more ought we to look to the fitness of him who aspires to be the lord and master of all priests! Yet how would it fare with us, if it should happen that the man most deficient in all these virtues, one so abject as not to be worthy of the lowest place among the priesthood, should be chosen to fill the highest place of all? What would you say of such a one, when you behold him sitting upon the throne glittering in purple and gold? Must he not be the "Antichrist, sitting in the temple of God, and showing himself to be God"?[2] Verily such a one lacketh both wisdom and charity; he standeth in the temple as an image, as an idol, from which as from dead marble you would seek counsel.

———

In one sense, the church during the Middle Ages was full of life. But not during the tenth century. Though there were some points of light and a multitude of fascinating individuals, a deep malaise in relation to the biblical gospel had established itself in the church. Christianity had become what it never was in essence—a structured, hierarchical state religion. Symptomatic of this was the symbiotic relationship that had developed between the emperor and the pope.

When the church begins to have power and influence not merely in society but over society, it tends to become more interested in its own voice being heard than in the word of the gospel being proclaimed. The decay of the church is never the fault of the world. Inward spiritual decline always precedes outward collapse.

Almost inevitably, when we come to the tenth century (900–1000) and the prospect of the second Christian millennium breaking upon the world, our expectations are aroused. Certainly, there were millennial expectations. But the tenth century was in some ways the epitome of the so-called Dark Ages. In fact, in one popular illustrated survey of church history, the chart that depicts the major events and personalities of each of the twenty centuries, for the tenth century lists . . . no people and no events.

The firmament was dark indeed. The church of Christ, although called to be the light of the world, was hiding the gospel. Called to be the salt of the earth, it had lost its saltiness (Matt. 5:13–16). Seeking glory in the things of earth, it no longer shone with the glory of heaven. Seeking power in this world, it had become weak in witness to that world.

Lord Acton famously wrote, "Power tends to corrupt, and absolute power corrupts absolutely."[3] The church had gained power. But the greater the power, the greater the corruption. And, sadly, those who were called to minister God's Word were increasingly ignorant of its truth.

The narrative is a salutary one, if only because there are signs in church life today that we have not yet learned from history. For what happened to the churches in the period preceding the new millennium in the tenth century has had an echo in modern church life: the church sought to convey an impressive message by building massive (and massively expensive) cathedrals; its worship was characterized by observation rather than participation; its communication of its message to the people took place through mystery plays rather than through biblical exposition in the local churches. It was led by superstars rather than ministers, individual leaders with their followers, some of whom desired more than anything else to be in the shoes of their leaders and to taste the same adulation.

Why the medieval mystery plays? Was it really because people were uneducated, unable to read Scripture, and therefore needed the gospel to be presented in visual form? That argument might have been more persuasive if the church had also trained its vast number of clergy to read, to understand, and to teach and preach the Scriptures. But many priests were themselves ignorant of the Word of God, and were therefore incapable of arresting the inherent decay in both church and society through the power of the gospel.

The buildings were—and many of them remain—magnificent edifices designed to create a sense of transcendence. Yet it was in part a papal church building program, with its attendant "capital campaign" fund-raising efforts that would prove to be the catalyst for the Reformation in the early sixteenth century.

And the worship? Ordinary people were spectators of ritual and audiences for music that might appeal to their aesthetic senses. But since they did not participate in the singing, did not hear Christ-centered biblical exposition and gospel-filled preaching, could not follow the Latin Mass, seldom received the bread and the wine, and were not permitted to serve the Lord's Supper to each other, to be present at a worship service was largely to be a mere spectator.

How unnerving, therefore, to see churches today with massive indebtedness for constructing hugely impressive church buildings, organizing services as though they were concerts, and apparently measuring the "quality of worship" by a grid appropriate to performance rather than faith. And, in most instances, either having no second service on the Lord's Day, or one that is vastly diminished in attendance. As we have already noted, it hardly seems to be rocket science to draw the conclusion that if the "quality of worship" is so remarkable, the participants would surely desire more, and as soon as possible. After all, doesn't the Recipient of the worship? How sad if all we are measuring is performance ratings.

As if this were not sufficiently discouraging, we are already on the way to creating superstar ministers whose spiritual success is measured by the size of the morning congregations who come to hear them. Magazine interviews with ministers are rarely with pastors who have served the same small congregation for thirty years, know and love every member, and faithfully feed and nourish them with a diet of biblical exposition and pastoral love. Rather, they are with "successful" ministers of congregations with memberships in the thousands. What the casual reader might easily fail to notice is that the credit lines often give the lie to the degree of "success." Dr. X, we read, is minister of a congregation of twelve thousand members. But elsewhere we discover that he preaches to seven thousand people every Sunday morning. Where, we are inclined to ask, are the missing five thousand? Does Dr. X find it difficult to sleep at night knowing he has the pastoral oversight of so many thousands who have professed Christ but decline to praise Him Sunday after Sunday? The "success" is in fact a massive burden that crushes the genuinely sensitive and faithful heart.

Sadly, we are already in an era in which public articles as well as professional individuals are available to enable ministers to "monetize" their ministry success.[4] It is all eerily medieval.

A classic illustration of how low the leadership of the church had sunk at the close of the first millennium is found in the papacy of Stephen VI (896–97).[5]

Stephen had his predecessor, Formosus (891–96), tried at a council in 897. Not content to do this with the accused absent, he had Formosus exhumed, dressed in papal robes, set up in a chair, tried, and found guilty. Then, having been stripped of his robes and having three fingers of his right hand removed (those used in pronouncing the benediction), Formosus' body was paraded through the streets of Rome to his unmarked grave. Several days later, he was again exhumed, and his mutilated body was thrown into the River Tiber. Stephen himself would later be imprisoned in Rome and strangled while he was there. But within a year, Formosus was headline news once again when he was reburied in St. Peter's.

In the one hundred years between 896 when Stephen had become pope and the beginning of the new millennium in 1000, no fewer than thirty popes and two antipopes (rival claimants to the papal chair) were elected. It is hardly surprising that serious believers were conscious that unless there was a reformation of the head of the church (the papacy), it would not be possible to reform the whole body.

Yet even under these circumstances, God does not leave Himself without a witness. There were bright lights. Among them were the Benedictine monks of the great Abbey of Cluny north of Lyons, France. Endowed in 910, the monastery developed a new spiritual discipline in the context of wholesale decline. The Rule of St. Benedict was practiced with a new integrity, and the monks were expected to engage in personal study of Scripture and prayer as well as in the corporate acts of worship and work in the abbey community. Simplicity in disciplined Christian living and a truer spirituality were the goal. By the end of the century, the foundations for the great abbey church had been laid, which after forty years of construction was the largest church in Christendom. It would last until the French Revolution.

Distinctive to Cluny was that it became the organizational center of an entire network of abbeys that followed its model. New abbots were appointed by the abbot of Cluny, which eventually made the occupant of that position one of the most powerful and important individuals in the entire church. All the more so since the monastic orders owed loyalty directly to the pope and not to any local bishop.

How striking that there should be a parallel to the condition of the professing church in the West at the beginning of the third millennium. In those days, men feared the old paganism and the coming of a spiritual night.

We may well share their fears. Rather than enhancing life, the rejection of the gospel has birthed political leadership without moral compass and spiritual backbone. Western governments national and local pour significant financial resources into trying to deal with the collapse of a sense of personal worth and purpose. School assembly halls boast banners encouraging pupils to "Trust in yourself." Commentators on our contemporary society, and not necessarily only Christians, are conscious that these are critical days. If the foundations are destroyed, what can the righteous do?

The only hope is if the light of the world shines, if the salt retains its saltiness. We do not share the perspective of the monastery. But one of the heartbeats of the Reformation message (especially in Calvin's teaching) was that it is possible to live out the aspirations of monasticism in the day-to-day world, to serve Christ in the power of the Spirit and in the fellowship of the church—that is, to live a life totally given over to the service of God in everything we do.

Throughout the history of the church, it has always been those who have given themselves to the simplicities of day-by-day devotion to Jesus Christ who have made the deepest and most enduring impression for Him in the world.

All Glory, Laud, and Honour

THEODOLPH OF ORLEANS (920)[6]

All glory, laud, and honour
to thee, Redeemer, King!
to whom the lips of children
made sweet hosannas ring.

Thou art the King of Israel,
thou David's royal Son,
who in the Lord's Name comest,
the King and Blessed One.

The company of angels
are praising thee on high;
and mortal men and all things
created make reply.

The people of the Hebrews
with palms before thee went;
our praise and prayer and anthems
before thee we present.

To thee before thy passion
they sang their hymns of praise;
to thee, now high exalted,
our melody we raise.

Thou didst accept their praises;
accept the prayers we bring,
who in all good delightest,
thou good and gracious King.

THE ELEVENTH CENTURY

SCHISM, ANSELM, AND THE CRUSADES

Anselm, archbishop of Canterbury, stands out in medieval theology for his remarkable exposition of the necessity of the incarnation and the nature of the atonement. In the text below, from **Cur Deus homo,** *he is in dialogue with his pupil Boso.*

Anselm. But this [i.e., satisfaction] cannot be effected, except the price paid to God for the sin of man be something greater than all the universe besides God.

Boso. So it appears.

Anselm. Moreover, it is necessary that he who can give God anything of his own which is more valuable than all things in the possession of God, must be greater than all else but God himself.

Boso. I cannot deny it.

Anselm. Therefore none but God can make this satisfaction.

Boso. So it appears.

Anselm. But none but a man ought to do this, otherwise man does not make the satisfaction.

Boso. Nothing seems more just.

Anselm. If it be necessary, therefore, as it appears, that the heavenly kingdom be made up of men, and this cannot be effected unless the aforesaid satisfaction be made, which none but God can make and none but man ought to make, it is necessary for the God-man to make it.

Boso. Now blessed be God! We have made a great discovery with regard to our question. Go on, therefore, as you have begun. For I hope that God will assist you.

Anselm. Now must we inquire how God can become man.

———

The halfway point in the story of the Christian church was marked and marred by the Great Schism.

We have already seen that the Eastern and Western churches, with their centers in Constantinople and Rome, respectively, not only employed different languages in writing theology and celebrating the liturgy but also had developed differently. In addition, each now had in place its own power structures, focused on the pope in Rome in the West and on the patriarch of Constantinople in the East. The tension between the two came to a climax in the middle of the eleventh century. Its presenting symptom was disagreement over the *filioque* clause. But closer examination reveals a more complex situation.

The Nicene Creed was the formal settlement of the controversy over the deity of Christ. It had simply stated that the Holy Spirit proceeds from the Father. But under the influence of Augustine of Hippo, the Western church had come to the conclusion that a fuller statement of biblical teaching was needed: the Spirit proceeds not only from the Father but also from the Son.

For Augustine, the Holy Spirit is the bond or expression of love between the Father and the Son. He must therefore "proceed" from both. Thus, the Father loves the Son in the Spirit, and the Son loves the Father in the Spirit. This love extends to believers by bringing us into communion with both the Father and the Son in the "fellowship of the Holy Spirit" (2 Cor. 13:14).

How could such a small, indeed apparently trivial, difference—the addition of the Latin suffix *que* (and)—create such a great schism?

More than a Suffix

We may well regret the sharp division that took place between Christians in this way. There can be little doubt that a powerful political agenda on both sides triumphed over any desire for visible unity. Yet it is also worth noting that neither party regarded the theological difference as either small or trivial. For those on the side of *filioque*, it was important to understand and express God's being as truly and fully as Scripture allows us. Indeed, put in its best light, love demands of us an accurate description of the

One we love. And, after all, we recognize that the addition of an iota makes all the difference in the world to the way the church described the Lord Jesus.[1] It is all too easy to imbibe the anti-intellectualism that has dominated evangelical Christianity over the past century or so and to regard as "scholastic" what the early Christians believed was an aspect of their devotion to God. But it betrays a deep spiritual inconsistency to do this if we ourselves pay close attention to the details of things that interest us personally (be they terms in music, statistics in baseball, the use of the English language, or computer terminology).

Why then, did the Western church insist on Augustine's view of the relationships of the Holy Spirit within the Trinity, and defend the doctrine of the double procession? There were several considerations:

- Jesus spoke of the Spirit as "proceeding from" ("going out from") and being sent by the Father (John 15:26). But Scripture encourages us to see what God does in history as a revelation of who He is in eternity. The Spirit is sent by the Father, but He is also sent by the Son (John 14:16, 26; 15:26). By parity of reasoning, therefore, the Spirit must also proceed from the Son, or the Son would lack the necessary authority to send Him.

- The Spirit is described as the Spirit *of* God the Father (Rom. 8:14; 1 Cor. 2:14; 3:16). But He is also the Spirit *of* the Son (Gal. 4:6). These genitives ("of") are surely parallel to each other. The Spirit is "of" the Son in the same way that He is "of" the Father. If "of" in relation to the Father means that the Spirit "proceeds" from Him, then the same must be true in relation to the Son.

- A further consideration here has to do with the logic of biblical theology. God has made Himself fully and finally known to us in Christ—insofar as our humanity can know Him. While the single procession doctrine is true (the Spirit does indeed proceed from the Father), it is not the whole truth. Otherwise, there would be an obvious but inexplicable gap in our knowledge of God: we would know how the Father relates to the Son and the Father to the Spirit in the Trinity. But we would not know how the Son and the Spirit relate to each other—if at all. We would, therefore, not really know God in terms of His intra-Trinitarian relations, despite the fact that we are invited into communion with God the Trinity.

There were, therefore—at least in the eyes of Western Christians—important theological reasons for adding the *filioque* clause. What, therefore, was the problem? Eastern Christians detected several, reminding us yet again that there is no theology without psychology.

Theological expositions and debates do not take place in purified and hermetically sealed intellectual vacuums. They always involve people. And people are always complex personalities with varied emotions, concerns, and ambitions. Even though theology is an activity of the mind—indeed, especially because it is an activity of the mind—it cannot be disassociated from the will, the emotions, and the motives of the fallen individual. There is no such thing as "pure theology," although those who engage in theological debate do not always take this into account.

So it was here.

Objections

One reason the Eastern church objected to the addition of the *filioque* clause was quite simple: the original form of the creed had been approved by an *ecumenical* council at Constantinople and expressed in the so-called Niceno–Constantinopolitan Creed of 381. In that sense, the worldwide church had agreed to this wording. But the *filioque* clause had been added by some Christians (in the West) without reference to the whole church. In that sense, it both ignored and threatened the important principle of the unity of the church for which the Lord Jesus prayed.

Such an objection is understandable and indeed in many respects quite justifiable. There was, however, also a deep theological issue at stake: two different ways of thinking about the Trinity had developed.

Eastern theologians had spoken about the Father as the fountain of the deity of the Trinity who as such guaranteed the unity of the three persons. In their view, such unity required that there should be a single fountain or source of the divine nature. Thus, to Eastern ears, saying that the Spirit proceeded from both the Father and the Son sounded as though Western Christians were claiming a dual *origin* for the Holy Spirit—as if both the Father and the Son acted as "father" to the Spirit.

In addition, there was a political dimension to the controversy.

Church Politics?

The Western church now held that the pope was the chief bishop of the church. As such, he was also the vicar or representative of Jesus Christ on earth. When this claim was set in the context of the *filioque* clause, it sounded to Eastern ears that the work of the Holy Spirit on earth was being virtually subordinated to the pope as well—after all, the pope was the vicar on earth of the One from whom that Spirit proceeded.

The bottom line of the discussion, as is often the case, thus became the issue of power and authority in the church, and also in the world. The fear of the Eastern church (by no means entirely misplaced) was that the Western church had in view exercising authority over the church in the East.

The protracted controversy led ultimately to the Great Schism of 1054. It gives us a glimpse of the way the church had become more interested in the theology of glory than the theology of the cross (as Martin Luther would later express it). It also helps us see why the Christian church has sometimes appeared to outsiders as more concerned with the power of its structures than with expressing the meekness and gentleness of its Lord and the saving power of the gospel.

The century of schism was also the century of a great theologian on the one hand and, on the other, a papal sermon that would leave a permanent mark on Christian theology and on world history.

The theologian was Anselm of Canterbury.

Anselm of Canterbury

Anselm (1033–1109) was one of the most significant theologians, if not the most significant, between Augustine and Thomas Aquinas. Italian by birth, he spent much of his earlier life at the monastery of Le Bec in Normandy. There, he was mentored by and eventually succeeded Lanfranc when the latter became archbishop of Canterbury (1063)—a position to which Anselm himself would later ascend in 1093.

Anselm was by any standards an extraordinary man, combining several striking qualities. He had backbone. On his appointment as archbishop of Canterbury, he refused to accept the pallium[2] from King William II (Rufus), the third son of William the Conqueror. He thus symbolically insisted that his office was not derived from, nor would his ministry be subject to, any secular authority.

Anselm also had brain power. He was hugely gifted intellectually, and is often described as the "Father of Scholasticism."

The term *scholastic* is often used in a demeaning, pejorative sense— dry, irrelevant, excessively and pedantically intellectual. But strictly speaking, it indicates only an approach to reality that involves serious thinking and careful and critical analysis, involving the development of concepts and technical language, and the use of clear and logical exposition of complex issues, expressed by carefully nuanced distinctions in thought—features of all reliable scholarly work.

What made Anselm so remarkable is the impact of his contribution on two major theological issues: philosophical arguments for the existence of God and the doctrine of the atonement.

Anselm and His Argument

Anselm's name is inextricably linked with what is known as the ontological argument for the existence of God. While it is probably the least familiar of the classical arguments for God's existence, it has probably held greater fascination for philosophers than any other.

Anselm argued that, logically, God must exist, since He is "that than which nothing greater can be conceived" (*aliquid quo maius nihil cogitari potest*).[4] Otherwise, He would not be the greatest conceivable being, since it would be possible to conceive of a greater being—namely, one than whom no greater can be conceived and who *in addition* actually exists. Therefore, Anselm concluded, God—defined as the One than whom no greater can be conceived—exists necessarily.

Many first-time readers of Anselm at this point instinctively feel like a novice chess player who hears his opponent saying "checkmate" after only four moves, and they wonder if some intellectual sleight of hand has taken place in this apparently simple argument.

The problem, of course, is that Anselm's starting place (God's being "the One than whom no greater can be conceived") already implies the existence of God, and therefore the argument only proves what it pre-supposes. The reasoning is circular. But the fact that something exists in the mind does not mean it necessarily exists in reality. Existence is not a necessary aspect of concept.[5]

It is worth remembering here that this and the other classical arguments for the existence of God—cosmological (the argument that there must be a first cause), teleological (the argument from design), moral (the argument from conscience and the universal sense of obligation), and historical (the argument from the universality of belief in God)—are not distinctively *biblical* or specifically Christian arguments. Thus, even if the arguments themselves are valid, they do not establish the specifically *Christian* claim that the God who exists is the One described in the pages of the Bible, the God who sent His Son to be the Savior. There remains a gap between the conclusion of these arguments and the revelation given in Scripture.

This is why such arguments seem to have been originally developed by Christians not so much as independent, logical arguments to be employed in convincing atheists but rather as ways of showing that Christian faith is intellectually coherent and not irrational.

Herman Bavinck expresses this well:

Whereas natural theology[6] was initially an account, in the light of Scripture, of what Christians can know concerning God from creation, it soon became an exposition of what nonbelieving rational persons could learn from nature by the power of their reasoning. In other words, natural theology became rational theology.[7]

This is all the more likely when we recognize that Anselm's *Proslogion*, in which he enunciates his ontological argument, is also an expression of his conviction that the knowledge of God involves *fides quaerens intellectum* (faith seeking understanding). Augustine's approach was similar. Thus, he urged his hearers, "*Crede ut intelligas*" (Believe so that you may understand).[7] This is not an appeal to sacrifice our intellects. It is an affirmation that we are dependent on God's self-revelation in order to know Him. That is the supreme use of the intellect, and the profoundest logic. We can understand God only in His own terms as He discloses Himself to us.[8] In the final analysis, we must always remember that all reasoning about God is dependent on His revelation.

Cur Deus Homo

Anselm's other great work was titled *Cur Deus homo* (Why did God become man? or Why the God-man?). In it, he employed what he called the *remoto Christo* principle. In essence, he sought to show the internal intellectual coherence of the gospel without direct reference to the narrative of the gospel—to show the logical coherence of the gospel without reference to the actual events of the life of Jesus.[9]

As with his ontological argument, Anselm was employing logical thinking in order to demonstrate how in the nature of the case salvation must be provided in a substitute. His own answer to his Latin question was this: we are sinners and we have dishonored God and His glory. We have a double problem: none of us is able to honor God as we ought to, nor can we pay back the debt that we already owe because we have dishonored Him; we remain, therefore, forever debtors. As such, we are obligated to pay our debt; but as bankrupts, none of us is capable of doing so.

How can this conundrum be solved? Man alone owes the debt and man alone must, but cannot, repay it. God provides the solution: in the person of His Son He took our flesh, wore our nature, lived a perfect life, and is able therefore to pay the debts of others by His death. God accomplished what we cannot do. Becoming man in Christ, He both honors God and pays the debt we owe to Him. The gospel thus—Anselm believed—has its own logical coherence and the death of Christ its own logical necessity and efficacy.

The book itself is in the form of a dialogue. One of its greatest moments occurs when Anselm's conversation partner (delightfully named Boso) is struggling to grasp precisely why the work of Christ is so essential. Anselm responds: "*Nondum considerasti, quanti ponderis sit peccatum*" (You have not yet considered the greatness of the weight of sin).[10] Of all Anselm's statements, this may be the one most worth committing to memory. It goes to the heart of many theological misunderstandings—of ourselves and of our sin, of divine election, of the wonder of the love of God, and of holiness. It is especially important when it comes to understanding the work of Christ for us. For only when we grasp the many-sided character and the depth of our sinfulness can we come to understand and appreciate the wonder of the multidimensional work of Jesus Christ for us.[11] And only then will we appreciate the absolute necessity for God's election, His pursuit of us through His Spirit, and His sovereign regeneration of us if we are ever to come to faith.

Anselm's other writings include his work on the Trinity, in which he defends the Augustinian doctrine of the double procession of the Spirit. Yet alongside much that is wonderfully impressive in Anselm, he was also a man of his (and his church's) time. He lived in the era in which sacraments had for all practical purposes begun to take the place of the Holy Spirit and tradition had displaced Scripture. In addition, Mary, instead of being merely a wonderful disciple who, through the ups and downs of her life, trusted Christ as Savior and Lord, had now developed a mediatorial function between sinners and the Savior. It is always a salutary thing to see the long-term effects of believing—as the Roman Catholic Church taught and continues to teach—that although there is only one source of divine revelation, it flows to us in two streams: sacred Scripture and sacred tradition. It is almost inevitable that at some point the latter will add to the former.

Anselm lived into the early years of the twelfth century. In 1109, as his life was clearly ending, he asked to be placed on ashes, stretched out before God on the floor. Whatever his inconsistencies, he wanted to die expressing his own consciousness of the greatness of the weight of sin, prostrated as a spiritual beggar before a gracious Savior.

Crusading Christianity?

The church's involvement in politics emerged once again in events that brought the eleventh century to a close.

On a late November day in 1095, Pope Urban II stood on a high platform in a field outside Clermont, France. Surrounded by a massive crowd of listeners, he preached a sermon that redirected the stream of history for two centuries. Its theme? A military crusade against the Islamic invasion and conquest of once-Christian areas of the world.

It is easy for us to comment that Jesus said, "My kingdom is not of this world" (John 18:36), and that the church's work is always "ministerial," not "political," an expression of the authority of God's Word applied in love to His people and with prophetic power to the world. In relationship to the world, the church is always an earthen vessel in which the gospel is contained, an army whose weapons are not of the flesh yet express divine power (2 Cor. 10:4).[12]

The First Crusade, and the wave of Crusades that continued until nearly the end of the thirteenth century, had in view the recapturing of the traditional "holy sites" of Christendom that had been conquered by the Muslim powers. To schoolchildren of an earlier generation (or was it only school*boys*?), mention of the Crusades conjured up stories of courage and romance and stereotyped pictures of Richard the Lionheart. Indeed, in the United Kingdom, there were evangelical organizations for young people called "Crusaders" whose badge was in the shape of a medieval shield with a red cross emblazoned on it. In more recent days, by contrast, there have been expressions of apology verging on repentance for such naming practices as well as for the Crusades themselves.

It is easy to forget that (whatever one's view of the church's involvement) what prompted the Crusades in the first place was the kind of abuse and widespread physical atrocities that today draw the condemnation of the United Nations and at times international military response.

Today, we would be deeply critical of church leaders' "preaching a crusade" of this kind as Pope Urban and indeed Bernard of Clairvaux did. But medieval Europe was a different world. The church and the state were interdependent. The fact of Christendom—the idea of a thoroughly Christian, transnational society—was taken for granted. In one sense, the pope was a kind of empowered secretary-general of the United Nations. Thus, a religious concern about human atrocities was activated through military power.

Doubtless, the gospel was unnecessarily sullied by the granting of indulgences to participants in the Crusades and perhaps by the prospect of worldly fame to be won in the name of Christ. But we would be shortsighted if we thought the Crusades were exclusively expressions of crass military imperialism. For what prompted the Crusades was Islamic military expansionism—the invasion of entire nations where the Christian faith had once flourished. As has happened again in our own time, Christians faced few alternatives, none attractive: conversion to Islam, flight from their homes, the payment of fines, second-rate citizenship, or death. No doubt, motives were mixed; trade routes and finances were at stake. But on the other hand, the Crusades involved massive financial expenditure and much sacrifice in their efforts to respond to the calls of beleaguered Christians for fellow believers in the West to come to their assistance.

We cannot avoid being citizens of two worlds. But we endanger the gospel if we confuse these two worlds. And doubtless, to some extent, this was true of the Crusades. While that is a matter for regret, a righteous desire to preserve the right to life, liberty, and pursuit of happiness of those who live in other nations, by military means if necessary, is a sentiment shared by many Christians today who believe there is such a thing as a "just war" even if it is a terrible necessity. In the case of the Crusades, more than one historian has judged that had the Christian West done nothing, far from enjoying the development of democracy in the centuries that followed, the West would consist today of Islamic states.

History, even where professing Christians are involved, is always messy.

All Hail, Adorèd Trinity!

ANONYMOUS ELEVENTH-CENTURY LATIN HYMN

(*AVE, COLENDA TRINITAS*)[13]

All hail, adorèd Trinity!
All hail, eternal Unity!
O God the Father, God the Son,
And God the Spirit, ever One.

Three Persons praise we evermore,
One only God our hearts adore:
In thy sure mercy ever kind
May we our strong protection find.

O Trinity! O Unity!
Be present as we worship thee;
And with the songs that angels sing
Unite the hymns of praise we bring.

12

THE TWELFTH CENTURY

THEOLOGICAL DEVELOPMENTS

Bernard of Clairvaux preached an extensive series of sermons on the Song of Solomon in which he employed allegorical application. He had reached only as far as Song of Solomon 1:3 when he preached his fifteenth sermon in the series, "On the Names of God, and the Name of Jesus." In the text below, he is commenting on the words "your name is oil poured out."

One thing, my brethren, I feel sure of, namely, that, if Philip and Andrew be the porters, we shall never meet with a repulse when we go begging for oil, when we want to see Jesus. . . . But what will Jesus answer? Doubtless the same which He spoke once before, "Unless the grain of wheat, falling into the ground, dieth, itself remaineth alone. But if it die, it bringeth forth much fruit." Therefore let the Divine Grain die that the crop of the gentiles may spring up. For "thus it behoveth Christ to suffer, and to rise again from the dead, and that penance and remission of sins should be preached in his name," not alone in Judaea, but throughout all nations; so that from the one name of Christ, countless millions of believers should be called Christians, and should exclaim in chorus, "Thy name is as oil poured out."

In this, that is, the name of Christ, I recognize the name which we read of in the prophet Isaias, "He shall call His servants by another name, in which he, that is blest upon the earth, shall be blessed in God, amen." O name of benediction! O oil everywhere poured out!

Do you ask how widely it is poured out? From heaven it overflowed to Judea, and from Judea through the world at large, so that from the whole earth the Church sends up the wondering cry, "Thy name is as oil poured out," "Poured out" in truth, since not only has it overrun heaven and earth but even the dwellers beneath the earth have been sprinkled therewith, "that in the name of Jesus every knee should bow, of those that are in heaven, on earth and under the earth and that every tongue should confess" and say, "Thy name is as oil poured out." Behold the name of Christ! Behold the name of Jesus! Both were infused into the angels. Both were effused upon men, upon those men, who like beasts, "had rotted in their filth," and they, these holy names, "saved men and beasts, as God hath multiplied his mercy." How precious this name, this oil! Yet how cheap, too. How cheap, and yet how salutary! Were it not cheap, it would not be poured out for one like me. Were it not salutary, it could not have saved me. I participate in the name; I participate also in the inheritance. I am a Christian; I am, therefore, the brother of Christ. If I am really what I am called, I am "the heir of God and a co-heir with Christ." . . .

But wherefore is it compared to oil? . . .

Unless you can suggest something better, I will say that the name of Jesus bears resemblance to oil in the threefold use to which the latter lends itself, namely, for lighting, for food, and for healing. It feeds the flame, it nourishes the flesh, it soothes pain. It is light, and food, and medicine. Consider now how the same properties belong to the Bridegroom's name. When preached, it gives light; when meditated, it nourishes; when invoked, it soothes and softens.

———

While armies of crusaders were marching east, new movements of a very different kind were emerging in the church in the West. For within the span of the twelfth century, several of the most influential theologians in the history of the church came to the fore. Moreover, the century also witnessed the development of two major institutions that would shape Western culture well into the future.

The first was the emergence of the universities.

The second was the founding of the Inquisition (later, in 1542, to be named the Holy Office) at the Synod of Tours in 1163. It aggressively sought to identify heretics, created a vast network of informers to do so, and employed torture when thought necessary (an action authorized in 1252 by the papal bull *Ad extirpanda*[1]). The "guilty" were handed over to the civil authorities for execution. The church therefore—at least officially—did not execute heretics.[2]

At the same time, the twelfth century was notable for a number of significant theologians. Anselm of Canterbury had lived into its first decade. The scholastic theological style of which he is often seen as the father lingered on even as the content of his own theology was debated.

School Theology

The late Middle Ages saw something of a revival of the life of the intellect in the Christian church in the context first of the great monasteries and then in the new universities of Europe. School theology always has strengths and weaknesses. Its strength lies in its intellectual rigor. Its weakness tends to lie in its distance from ordinary church life. Thus, as theologians pressed toward the boundary fences of revealed knowledge, sometimes they asked questions that Scripture was clearly not designed to answer:

- When exactly did Adam sin? (Alexander of Hales[3] famously worked out that it must have been at 3 p.m., the hour when Christ died.)
- Could God have become a woman?
- Will Adam have all his ribs in the resurrection?

Discussions on the nature of angelic beings stretched to such questions as:

- Can two or more angels occupy the same space (hence the interest in how many angels can dance on a pin head)?

These questions indicate the extent to which school theology had moved increasingly in the direction of abstraction and speculation. It is perhaps not surprising then that the greatest of the scholastic theologians, such as Anselm and (as we shall see) Thomas Aquinas, also had a strong mystical streak that balanced their tendency to abstractions.

Peter Abelard

Others in the twelfth century have made a lasting impression on the story of theology. These include the brilliant but wayward Pierre du Pallet, better known as Peter Abelard (1079–1142). His autobiographical reflections bore the ominous but easily translated title *Historia calamitatum* (The history of my calamities).

"Feisty" might be the best word to describe Abelard. He seems to have criticized, fallen out with, opposed, or domineered almost everyone who knew him. At one stage, he went to study with Anselm of Laon (died 1117), a biblical scholar, but, disappointed with his teaching, he not only disrupted his lectures but also took the less-than-sensitive step of holding his own classes.[4] Indeed, Abelard possessed this spiritual and personal insensitivity to such a degree that seven years after he had become abbot of St. Gildas in Brittany in 1125, it seems that his own monks attempted to murder him (literally).

Today Abelard is perhaps best known for his relationship with his private student Heloise, with whom he fathered a child. He subsequently married her, and then maintained an extended correspondence while they lived separately (she in a nunnery). Not only in his personal life, but also in theological terms, he stands at the opposite end of the spectrum from Anselm of Canterbury.

Abelard's most famous work was titled *Sic et non* (Yes and no). It is a list of 158 questions discussed by the church's theologians. Many of them deal with basic theological issues: Does God's foreknowledge determine future events (question 27)? Others focused on ethical issues, including some that continue to trouble ethicists today, such as question 155: "A person is allowed to kill himself . . . or not." Some, however, raised issues that appear today to be "scholastic" and speculative in the pejorative sense: "The hour of the night the Lord rose from the dead is undetermined . . . or not."[5]

It is with Abelard's name that the so-called Abelardian or moral influence view of the atonement is often associated. He argued essentially that we are saved by the effect of the overwhelming love that the cross demonstrates, and not by Christ's paying any debt we might owe. In this sense—over against Anselm's teaching—the atonement terminates on mankind, not on God. It is in this way, to borrow and apply the words of Isaac Watts' famous hymn, that when "I survey the wondrous cross on which the Prince of Glory died. . . . Love so amazing, so divine, demands my soul, my life, my all." In a nutshell, Abelard held that through Christ, God more fully binds us to Himself in love—with the result that we become willing to do anything for Him. But such theological constructions have never been able to explain satisfactorily how the cross is an atonement.

These contrasting views were to dominate discussion on the atonement throughout the coming centuries, and they continue to do so today.

Anselm, of course, had died by the time Abelard wrote and was unable to reply. But caught up in debate with Abelard was a figure altogether better known in the church at large chiefly because his name has appeared in so many hymnbooks—Bernard of Clairvaux (1090–1153). We know him best for his rich expressions of the grace and love of the Lord Jesus Christ.

Bernard of Clairvaux

Bernard founded the monastery at Clairvaux in 1115 and from there exercised an influence in the church second only to the pope. He was renowned for his phenomenal knowledge of Scripture and his deep-seated devotion to Christ. It is not surprising to hear him say in one of his famous sermons on the Song of Solomon (on which his eighty-six extant sermons reached only chapter three, verse one!), "This is my philosophy, to know Jesus Christ and him crucified." For Bernard, the cause of love for God is the substitutionary work of Christ. The love that it effects is faith in its highest form.

But there was another side to *Doctor Mellifluus* (honey flowing), as Bernard came to be known. He was an enthusiast for the Crusades. Yet he viewed the life of the monastery as the highest and clearest indication of spiritual commitment. And while Martin Luther could later say that Bernard loved Jesus as much as anyone can,[6] on the other hand, his contemporary and friend Peter the Venerable, the abbot of Cluny, once wrote to him, "You perform all the difficult religious duties: you fast, you watch, you suffer; but you will not endure the easy ones—you do not love." Was this mainly a comment on the strength of Bernard's opposition to what he perceived to be false teaching? He was so vigorously opposed to Abelard's thought that he wrote to Pope Innocent III that in trying to show that Plato was a Christian, Abelard simply showed himself to be a pagan.[7]

The flowering of scholasticism was marked by the work of Peter of Lombardy (1095–1169).[8]

Peter Lombard

Peter arrived in Paris in the late 1130s, where he probably heard the lectures of Peter Abelard. He came to public attention through his commentary on Paul's letters, and toward the end of his life was appointed archbishop of Paris. His chief claim to fame lies in his—to us, quaintly titled—*Four Books of Sentences*. The Latin *sententiae* here means "views," "opinions," or "expositions" (i.e., not "sentences").

Peter worked his way systematically through the doctrines of the Christian faith, probing it all the time to ask questions about how we understand the gospel.[9] So comprehensive were the *Sentences* that they became part of the required program of studies in the University of Paris, and writing a commentary on it became essential preparation for a doctorate in theology. Somewhere in the region of 250 extant commentaries on the *Sentences* have been catalogued.[10]

What do we learn then from the twelfth century? In it, we encounter men of remarkable gifts and devotion. Here were theological visionaries. Yet almost all we know about serious Christianity takes us into the cloistered world of abbeys and nunneries and among those who spent their time studying, praying, and thinking. That trilogy should never be downplayed. The major "advance" of the church, however, appears to have been militaristic rather than evangelistic—Crusades in which the weapons of this world were used rather than the proclamation of the gospel, which is the sword of the Spirit.[11]

How sad that the Christian church in this period of history should be better known for its successes and failures with the sword rather than with the gospel. It is another great lesson to us never to allow the agenda or even the style of the world to determine the agenda or the lifestyle of the Christian church.

We make that mistake over and over again, personally as well as ecclesiastically. We need to learn again to bow at the feet of Jesus as our example as well as our Redeemer and adopt His countercultural lifestyle. He has set us in the world to witness to it, and there we must remain until we take our leave of it.

Jesus, Thou Joy of Loving Hearts

BERNARD OF CLAIRVAUX[12]

Jesus, Thou Joy of loving hearts,
Thou Fount of life, Thou Light of men,
From the best bliss that earth imparts,
We turn unfilled to Thee again.

Thy truth unchanged hath ever stood;
Thou savest those that on Thee call;
To them that seek Thee Thou art good,
To them that find Thee all in all.

We taste Thee, O Thou living Bread,
And long to feast upon Thee still;
We drink of Thee, the Fountainhead,
And thirst our souls from Thee to fill.

Our restless spirits yearn for Thee,
Where'er our changeful lot is cast;
Glad when Thy gracious smile we see,
Blessed when our faith can hold Thee fast.

O Jesus, ever with us stay,
Make all our moments calm and bright;
Chase the dark night of sin away,
Shed o'er the world Thy holy light.

13

———

THE THIRTEENTH CENTURY

FRANCIS AND THOMAS

In the text below, excerpted from his Summa Theologica, *Thomas Aquinas discusses aspects of the atonement with his characteristic probing of every angle.*

Objection 1: It would seem that Christ's Passion did not bring about our salvation by way of atonement [*per modum satisfactionis*]. For it seems that to make the atonement [*satisfacere*] devolves on him who commits the sin; as is clear in the other parts of penance [*in aliis poenitentiae*], because he who has done the wrong must grieve over it and confess it. But Christ never sinned, according to 1 Pt. 2:22: "Who did no sin." Therefore He made no atonement [*non satisfecit*] by His personal suffering.

Objection 2: Further, no atonement is made [*nulli satisfit*] to another by committing a graver offense. But in Christ's Passion the gravest of all offenses was perpetrated, because those who slew Him sinned most grievously, as stated above [question 47, article 6]. Consequently it seems that atonement could not be made to God by Christ's Passion.

Objection 3: Further, atonement [*satisfactio*] implies equality with the trespass, since it is an act of justice. But Christ's Passion does not appear equal to all the sins of the human race, because Christ did not suffer in His Godhead, but in His flesh, according to 1 Pt. 4:1: "Christ therefore having suffered in the flesh." Now the soul, which is the subject of sin, is of greater account than the flesh. Therefore Christ did not atone for our sins by His Passion (*Non ergo Christus sua passio satisfecit pro peccatis nostris*).

On the contrary, It is written [Ps. 69:4] in Christ's person: "Then did I pay that which I took not away." But he has not paid who has not fully atoned [*qui perfecte non satisfecit*]. Therefore it appears that Christ by His suffering has fully atoned [*satisfecerit perfecte*] for our sins.

I answer that, He properly atones [*satisfacit*] for an offense who offers something which the offended one loves equally, or even more than he detested the offense. But by suffering out of love and obedience, Christ gave more to God than was required to compensate for the offense of the whole human race. First of all, because of the exceeding charity from which He suffered; secondly, on account of the dignity of His life which He laid down in atonement, for it was the life of one who was God and man; thirdly, on account of the extent of the Passion, and the greatness of the grief endured, as stated above [question 46, article 6]. And therefore Christ's Passion was not only a sufficient but a superabundant atonement [*satisfactio*] for the sins of the human race; according to 1 Jn. 2:2: "He is the propitiation for our sins: and not for ours only, but also for those of the whole world."

Reply to Objection 1: Suffering, as such, is caused by an outward principle: but inasmuch as one bears it willingly, it has an inward principle.

Reply to Objection 2: Christ's love was greater than His slayers' malice; and therefore the value of His passion in atoning [*satisfacere sua passione*] surpassed the murderous guilt of those who crucified Him; so much so that Christ's suffering was sufficient and superabundant atonement [*ad satisfaciendum*] for His murderers' crime.

Reply to Objection 3: The dignity of Christ's flesh is not to be estimated solely from the nature of flesh, but also from the Person assuming it—namely, inasmuch as it was God's flesh, the result of which was that it was of infinite worth.

———

Martin Luther developed a striking way of describing the condition of the late medieval church as an organization. He believed it had been more interested in what he called *theologia gloriae*—a theology of the church's glory and power in the world—than it was with *theologiae crucis*—a theology of the cross. The church's quest for external splendor, professedly as an expression of the glory of God, had usurped the gospel in which that glory shines most brightly.

The whole church can be thankful that there were figures who pointed back to the teaching of Christ and the Apostles. Among those who did so in the thirteenth century was Francesco Bernardone. Given the baptismal name of Giovanni (John), he is better known to posterity as Francis of Assisi.

Francis of Assisi

Francis was born in Assisi in central Italy in 1182, and died some forty-four years later in 1226. He seems to have lived carelessly throughout his teens. He served in the army of Assisi until he was twenty-two but then took ill. The experience precipitated a spiritual crisis that led to a transformation in his view of life in general and of his own life in particular.

In 1209, in response to Jesus' words to His Apostles in Matthew 10, Francis dedicated himself to a life marked by Christlike devotion to the poor and the marginalized. He chose simplicity of lifestyle over against pomp and circumstance, and love for fellow Christians and for the lost in distinction from the use of the sword and the quest for glory. He was concerned to point the church back to its spiritual foundations and to illustrate a manner of life that pointed people to Christ. The rule he composed for the little community of brothers he gathered around himself was based on the Gospel passages that commended this lifestyle (see Matt. 16:24–26; 19:21; Luke 9:1–6).

There are different kinds of "intelligence." Some individuals appear to be able to grasp matters of enormous intellectual complexity; others see all reality in a stark, unsophisticated way, reduced to its absolute basics. Francis belonged to the latter category. He wanted to be "married" to Lady Poverty, walk hand in hand with Sister Charity, and to

serve as though he were the privileged praise leader of all creation—
hence his famous Canticle of the Sun. When truncated, as they often are,
Francis' views are presented as though he were a prototype of a new-age
individual seeking to be in tune with Mother Earth (to whom he refers,
but clearly in metaphorical fashion). But what is almost always omitted
from his canticle is its closing words:

> Woe to him who dies in mortal sin!
> Blessed are those who are found walking by your most holy will.
> The second death shall have no power to do them harm.
> Praise and bless the Lord, and give thanks to him.
> Serve him with great humility.

What Francis envisaged for the order he founded, the *Fratres Minores*
(the Lesser Brothers), was a fellowship of like-minded men devoted to
what he saw as the basic principles of the gospel. It was not to be, however. The order, including Francis himself, came under the authority of
a minister-general, Pietro de Catana, appointed by Cardinal Ugolino.[1]
Papal authority thus threatened the untutored free spirit of the new
community.

Francis remained a loyal son and servant of the Roman Catholic
Church. To a biblically instructed mind, it seems deeply paradoxical that
his simple and radical—one might say unsophisticated—application
of Christ's words to the Apostles was married to an acceptance of such
radically unbiblical teaching as the offering of plenary indulgences. Yet
Francis persuaded Pope Honorarius III to grant such indulgences to any
pilgrim visiting his chapel between Vespers on August 1 and August 2
each year. It is a consolation to know that during the last week of his life,
he had his companions read Psalm 142 repeatedly to him:

> With my voice I cry to the Lord
> With my voice I plead for mercy to the Lord. . . .
> I cry to you, O Lord;
> I say "You are my refuge,
> My portion in the land of the living."

The Dumb Ox of Aquino

Just as the life of the uneducated Francis of Assisi was drawing to a close, less than two hundred miles away, in the castle of Roccasecca, near Aquino, was born one of the most influential intellectuals of the Christian era—Thomas Aquinas. Born in 1225, he died in 1274, leaving behind a vast body of literature (reputedly, he could keep five secretaries at work simultaneously).

Thomas was by nature and instinct quiet and shy, yet of substantial build. So much so that at school and college he was known as "the dumb ox." Self-expression and publicly expressing personal opinions—the false virtues of the early twenty-first century—were absent from his disposition.

Although his family planned a legal career for him, the young Thomas set his heart on the religious life. While his family sought to divert him from his path, he remained committed to his religious quest. Thus, in 1244, he became a Dominican, spent some time in Paris, and then in 1248 moved to Cologne to become a student of the great Aristotelian scholar Albertus Magnus.[2] Further residence in Paris followed in 1252, and four years later he received his license to teach. During most of the decade from 1259, he was back in his homeland teaching. Once again, he returned to Paris until in 1272 he was appointed to head up a new Dominican House of Studies in Naples. Summoned to the Council of Lyons in 1274, he died en route.

From the outside, his life seems to have been cloistered, uneventful, and routine. Thomas, however, inhabited a massive world of the intellect. He is best known for two major works. The first, commonly known as the *Summa contra Gentiles* (sometimes called *A Summary of the Christian Faith*, although Thomas himself may have intended for it to be called *On the Truth of the Catholic Faith*[3])—was written between 1259 and 1264 as a manual for the use of missionaries in Spain. Here he attempts to help his fellow Christians defend and explain the intellectual coherence of the gospel, especially in the context of Islamic thought, which had been influenced by Aristotle—on whose works Thomas himself had written a large number of commentaries. He was committed to demonstrating that the Christian faith is an expression of the truest reasoning.

Thomas devoted some eight years to writing his yet more famous (although unfinished) *Summa Theologiae* (often *Theologica*), or *The Sum of Theology*. Set in the form of detailed questioning analysis, it summarizes the content of the Christian faith. In addition, he wrote philosophical studies and also gave expository lectures on Scripture. Like a number of the great theologians of the church, his output was so massive that ever since his death there have been disagreements about the "real teaching" of Thomas. Despite this, he became the guiding theologian of Roman Catholicism.

Thomas is perhaps best known in the church at large for relating Aristotle's categories of "substance" and "accidents" of objects to the mystery of the presence of Christ in the Lord's Supper. This distinction came to be seen as the clue to explaining the Roman Catholic view that the bread and wine of the Mass retain the appearance (the "accidents") of bread and wine while actually becoming the body and blood of Christ (in "substance"). Thus, at least for Thomas, right philosophy and right theology not only belong together, but the former can be a helpful handmaiden to the latter.

Thomas also famously held that right reason leads logically to the conclusion of God's existence (hence the "proofs" for the existence of God).[4] He stood in a theological tradition that can be traced back to Irenaeus and held that the distinction between the image and likeness of God (see Gen. 1:26–27) means that although through the fall we have lost our likeness to God, we retain the image in terms of our free will and our ability to reason rightly. In this sense, perhaps the most fundamental criticism of Thomas could be expressed by borrowing Anselm's words to Boso: *Nondum considerasti, quanti ponderis sit peccatum*—you have not yet considered how great the weight of sin is.[5]

This notwithstanding, Thomas was a man of extraordinary vision as well as ability and simplicity.[6] Indeed, driving him was a lifelong quest to behold God. It is remarkable, therefore, that at the end of his life he laid his work aside. He left his *Summa* unfinished. According to his friend and confessor Reginald of Piperno, when asked why, Thomas eventually replied: "I adjure you by the living Almighty God, and by the faith you have in our order, and by charity that you strictly promise me you will never reveal in my lifetime what I tell you. Everything that I have written seems to me to be chaff by comparison with those things that I have seen and have been revealed to me."

The Apostle Paul once wrote that by comparison with the privilege of knowing Christ, everything else is refuse or rubbish (Phil. 3:8). He did not despise the world, or learning, or literature. His point was one of comparison. We should not imagine Thomas thought all of his work was worthless and that he had wasted his time. But, especially for those who have reservations and concerns about the unbiblical nature of some of his teaching, how encouraging to think that, at the end—perhaps like Anselm and Francis—Thomas also realized more fully than ever before that Christ alone was his hope for the world to come.

The work of Thomas Aquinas is not always inspiring to read. Yet there is something inspiring in seeing a man seeking to develop, discipline, and use the gifts he has been given to help the church, to extend God's kingdom, and to express his devotion to Christ. Therein lies the challenge of Thomas' life.

All Creatures of Our God and King

Francis of Assisi

All creatures of our God and King
Lift up your voice and with us sing,
Alleluia! Alleluia!
Thou burning sun with golden beam,
Thou silver moon with softer gleam

    O praise Him! O praise Him!
    Alleluia! Alleluia! Alleluia!

Thou rushing wind that art so strong
Ye clouds that sail in Heaven along,
O praise Him! Alleluia!
Thou rising moon, in praise rejoice,
Ye lights of evening, find a voice!

Thou flowing water, pure and clear,
Make music for thy Lord to hear,
O praise Him! Alleluia!
Thou fire so masterful and bright,
That givest man both warmth and light.

Dear mother earth, who day by day
Unfoldest blessings on our way,
O praise Him! Alleluia!
The flowers and fruits that in thee grow,
Let them His glory also show.

And all ye men of tender heart,
Forgiving others, take your part,
O sing ye! Alleluia!
Ye who long pain and sorrow bear,

Praise God and on Him cast your care!
And thou most kind and gentle Death,
Waiting to hush our latest breath,
O praise Him! Alleluia!
Thou leadest home the child of God,
And Christ our Lord the way hath trod.

Let all things their Creator bless,
And worship Him in humbleness,
O praise Him! Alleluia!
Praise, praise the Father, praise the Son,
And praise the Spirit, Three in One!

14

THE FOURTEENTH CENTURY

FORERUNNERS OF THE
REFORMATION

John Wycliffe began life as a scholar and as a result of his studies realized that the teaching of the church had not been derived from the teaching of Scripture. The text below is excerpted from **On the Eucharist.**

Since, therefore, we cannot deny that the sacrament is broken, as the custom of the Church teaches (the senses will otherwise be led astray, through false reasonings based upon the truth), and the body of Christ is not broken, it is clear that the sacrament which is broken is not the body of Christ, because otherwise to the inquirer what is broken would be less truly spoken of as the body of Christ: what indeed he seeks is the substance of the thing.

The third objection they make is this, that unless the consecrated host is the body of Christ, we would not see nor eat the body of Christ, that is, we do not bite it with the teeth, and thus we would not receive it. Such a conclusion would be embarrassing for Christians.

But here we reply by distinguishing two kinds of seeing, of eating, and of digesting: namely, corporeal and spiritual. Thus we agree that we do not see the body of Christ in that sacrament with the bodily eye, but rather with the eye of the mind, that is, in faith through a mirror darkly. And just as the image is perfect in every part of the mirror, so that it can be seen either in part or completely by any bodily eye placed anywhere, so also should one believe in part concerning the body of Christ in the consecrated host as in a mirror. And in the same manner it is said that we do not physically touch or seize the body of Christ, just as we do not eat it corporeally. And this is the meaning of the hymn of the Church which sings,

> What thou canst not take nor see
> Faith yet affirms courageously,
> Beyond the things of sense.

Nor do we crush the body of Christ with the teeth, but rather we receive it in a spiritual manner, perfect and undivided. And so we understand the same hymn in which we sing,

> The thing within sustains no tear;
> The sign alone is broken there;
> No loss the state nor size doth bear
> Of this, the Signified.

But at this point certain folk object concerning our views that these ideas should not be mentioned to laymen who cannot understand or observe them, since from such ideas they might lose their former faith. But nothing is more absurd than such an objection; for entirely too many laymen as well as clergy are so unfaithful in this matter that they believe, worse than pagans, that the consecrated host is their God. Then, of course, they arrive at the aforesaid pagan arguments. Therefore, he who does not understand these matters ill understands the belief in the Trinity or the incarnation. Nor is the above mentioned lay belief pleasing to the Lord of Truth, but the vilest disbelief because it is a form of idolatry whereby a creature, cast down rather than lifted up, is worshiped as God.

If a vote were to be taken for "the man of the fourteenth century," a very strong candidate would be the Englishman John Wycliffe.[1] A Yorkshire man, born around 1330, he studied at the University of Oxford and became master of Balliol College. He was soon to become one of the most powerful forerunners of what we now know as the Reformation.

Like other major reformers, Wycliffe first devoted himself to a life of scholarship but became increasingly concerned about corruption in the church.[2] He argued that *dominium* (secular power and the possession of lands) represented a worldliness that had no place in the spiritual community of the Christian church. Since this emphasis was also naturally attractive to the nobility—rivals with the church, and eager to abrogate power and lands for themselves—to that extent he was given a certain degree of "protection" in the face of mounting ecclesiastical opposition to his influence and enjoyed a measure of freedom to teach and preach.

But this unbiblical feature of church life was simply the tip of the iceberg for him. His deeper concern was the distortion of biblical teaching as well as of the gospel lifestyle evident in the church.

In particular, Wycliffe placed special emphasis on the centrality, authority, and inerrancy of Scripture. As a result, he decried the authority of the pope (arguing that he had no more authority than any other minister), the activity of bishops (arguing that they were meant to be preachers and pastors first and foremost), and the practice of indulgences and confession to a priest (affirming that only the gospel brings pardon and deliverance from the power and penalty of sin). In addition, he repudiated the doctrine of transubstantiation as unbiblical, impossible, and offensive. While we do not find in Wycliffe a Luther-like announcement of justification by faith alone as the article of a standing or falling church, he certainly denied human merit and saw faith in Christ as the only way to life.

Increasingly, therefore, Wycliffe spoke, wrote, and encouraged others to preach about the authentic message of Scripture. His followers, who dressed like preaching monks in russet cassocks, became known as Lollards. The term, which implies that they were "babblers," was—like the later term *Puritan*—intended as a form of abuse. But gospel reality carries its own testimony, and it is widely thought that Wycliffe (and perhaps his followers) became the model for Geoffrey Chaucer's famous description of the parson in his *Canterbury Tales*:

> A good man was there of religioun
> And was a povre persoun [poor parson] of a toon
> But riche he was of hooly thought and werk.
> He was also a lerned man, a clerk,
> That Criste's gospel trewely wolde preche;
> His parisshens devoutly wolde he teche. . . .
>
> This noble ensample to his sheep he yaf [gave]
> That first he wroughte, and afterward he taughte . . .
> But Criste's loore [love], and His apostles twelve
> He taughte, but first he folwed it hymselve.

Wycliffe was, above all, a man of the Bible. His sense of its authority and its role as the Word of God to guide us on the way to heaven was palpable. His passion was to see it translated into English and let loose and available throughout England.[3] His teachings were condemned by the papacy. But the reach of his influence and the extent to which he blazed a trail that others would follow is underlined by the—appalling—fact that after his death his bones were dug up, burned, and then thrown into the River Swift. But as one historian wrote, from that river his ashes ran into the River Avon, and from there they flowed into the River Severn, and then into the seas and oceans, and thus to the rest of the world.

Wycliffe was a man with a passion that the Bible might be read and understood by everyone. In one sense, his memory is an inspiration to evangelical Christians. But the story of this "Morning Star of the Reformation" (as he came to be known) also causes us to look away in shame. Most Christians own not only one translation and copy of the Bible but several. Meanwhile, numbers of languages and dialects have little or no Scripture.[4] And we who have many copies, do we read them with the devotion and sense of privilege that we should?

If we learn anything from Wycliffe's life, we must learn the importance of getting the Word of God into the hands of people and explaining its message simply and clearly to them.

Jan Hus

Among the many lives influenced by Wycliffe's life and writings was that of Jan Hus of Bohemia (in the modern-day Czech Republic).

Hus was born in poverty in Husinec, Bohemia, around 1371, and he died in 1415. In 1402, while still a young man, he was appointed rector of the University of Prague.

Hus had been particularly moved by a cartoon he had seen illustrating the differences between the Roman Catholic Church and New Testament Christianity. It depicted two figures. One was the Lord Jesus Christ, the other the Roman pontiff: Jesus was wearing a crown of thorns; the pope was wearing a crown of gold. Hus asked himself this question: How can it be that the followers of someone who wore a crown of thorns so proudly wear a crown of gold?

The cartoon evoked in Hus the concern that Luther would take to its logical (and biblical) conclusion: the church was pursuing the theology of glory, not the theology of the cross. It was, in the end, a contradiction of Jesus' teaching. After all, Jesus had emphasized that the greatest of all is the one who is willing to be the servant of all (Matt. 20:26).

As he studied Scripture alongside the writings of Wycliffe and others, Hus was strengthened in his conviction that the church needed a radical reformation. Like the man born blind described in the Gospels, and indeed like the later Reformers, he did not see everything clearly all at once or repudiate everything the church taught. But he did grasp the importance of placing himself under the authority of the Scriptures, and this conviction was increasingly expressed and applied in his preaching. He drew heavily on the writings of Wycliffe. In due course, his own works were banned, and efforts were made to silence him. In 1411, he was excommunicated, persecuted, and then prosecuted. He was "a despiser of the keys"—having preached that a pope who did not submit to the authority of Scripture held no legitimate authority over believers.

When commanded to repudiate his writings, he responded that if he could be shown from the New Testament where they were in error, he would gladly do so.

Hus was granted a "safe conduct" in order to attend a major church council at Constance. When he arrived, it was clear that the "safe conduct" was a ploy to try, convict, and condemn him. The council commanded him to recant, which he courageously refused to do.

On July 6, 1415, Jan Hus was brought to the cathedral of Constance dressed in his priest's robes. Allowed no defense, he had his garments torn from him, and his tonsure was completely shaved—thus he was "defrocked" from his earlier ordination. A paper crown with demons portrayed on it was placed on his head and he was forced to watch the public burning of his own books before he himself was chained to a stake to be burned to death. He was heard to pray Stephen-like: "Lord Jesus, it is for you that I endure this cruel death with patience. Have mercy on my enemies, I pray." He died reciting the Psalms.

The name *Hus*, as its sound suggests, means "goose." Often taunted that he was indeed a silly goose, he is said to have responded with prophetic insight: "God has sent among you just a silly goose, but one day he will send among you an eagle." It was Erasmus of Rotterdam who was later charged with having "laid the egg that Luther hatched" (to which he replied that he had "expected a different kind of bird"). But it might be nearer the truth to say that it was the egg of the goose that Martin Luther fully hatched.

Hus left behind a large number of followers who effected important reformations of church life: the free preaching of Scripture, receiving both the bread and the wine at Communion, ending clerical amassing of wealth, and the outlawing of simony.[5] All of this kept many of them within the pale of the church, although others turned their backs on it and formed themselves into the *Unitas Fratrum* (union of brothers), some of whom eventually would develop into the Moravians, who in the eighteenth century had a great influence on the Wesley brothers. Others would later be attracted to the Reformed churches.

The plotline of this book is found in Jesus' words "I will build my church and the gates of hell shall not prevail against it." He did not say, "The gates of hell will not attack it," but that they "shall not prevail." This was the conviction of both Wycliffe and Hus and of those who looked to their example and leadership. From one point of view, their lives may have seemed wasted—despised, attacked, persecuted, and, in the case of Hus, even martyred. Some of those who supported them vanished like the morning dew. But these two men were faithful to the point of death, unyielding to the power of the church only because they had yielded first to Jesus Christ. Their hope and prayer was that after their deaths the church of Jesus Christ would experience a mighty renewal—their prayers were heard and answered.

We seek to be faithful to Jesus Christ. We may not see the fruit of that faithfulness. But we do not live or die to ourselves but to Christ. The gates of hell cannot keep us down. As we carry gospel seed, we may feel tears in our eyes because there seems to be so little fruit. But if we do not live to see the harvest, others will. Jesus has promised, and that is enough for us. Those who sow in tears will reap with shouts of joy. Those who are steadfast and immovable will always be abounding in the work of the Lord. Their labor is not in vain (Ps. 126:5; 1 Cor. 15:58).

There Comes a Galley, Laden

JOHN TAULER (C. 1300–1361)

There comes a galley, laden
Up to the highest board;
She bears a heav'nly burthen,
The Father's eterne Word.

She saileth on in silence,
Her freight of value vast:
With Charity for mailsail,
And Holy Ghost for mast.

The ship has dropt her anchor,
Is safely come to land;
The Word eterne, in likeness
Of man, on earth doth stand.

At Bethlem in a stable,
To save the world forlorn
(O bless Him for His mercy),
Our Saviour Christ is born.

And whosoe'er with gladness
Would kiss Him and adore,
Must first endure with Jesus
Great pain and anguish sore.

Must die with Him moreover,
And rise in flesh again,
To win that life eternal,
Which doth to Christ pertain.

15

THE FIFTEENTH CENTURY
SETTING THE STAGE

Girolamo Savonarola is one of the most enigmatic and dramatic figures among the forerunners of the Reformation. The text below is excerpted from his **The Triumph of the Cross.**

Man could not, of himself, atone for sin. Only God, who had never sinned, could make fitting satisfaction for it. Therefore He, in His infinite mercy, wisdom, and power, willed, by becoming man, to pay the debt which man owed, and was unable to pay.

Man owed satisfaction, and God-made Man alone had power to make that satisfaction, not indeed for Himself, but for the whole human race. In this fact is revealed the fitness of His Incarnation, wherein He has united the Divine to the Human nature. In this mystery we behold His power, His wisdom, and the goodness whereby He has wholly given Himself to the human race, to embrace it, and to draw it to His love. But, above all His other attributes, His mercy is made manifest; for it has led Him to be crucified for love of us. His justice also is seen; for He has Himself made satisfaction for original sin. Hence, while His mercy should inspire repentant sinners with the surest hope, His justice should cause the impenitent to tremble.

This is the reason why, since the coming of Christ into the world, so many men have been drawn from sin to holiness of life.

When we consider these mercies, and the innumerable other benefits conferred by Christ upon human nature, we discover depths of wisdom which are unfathomable by the intellect of man, and which, for this very reason, are accounted folly by the world. We see, moreover, how fitting it was that Christ should suffer for the guilt of mankind.

But since He came, not merely to suffer for man, but likewise to set him an example of righteous living, it behoved Him to choose a most bitter and disgraceful death; thus teaching us that neither shame, nor suffering, should force us to betray the cause of truth and justice.

Time forbids me to enlarge upon the other reasons which caused our Saviour to choose His terrible mode of death. I will only add, that His cross has been, to them that love Him, a fount of sweetness and of light, known only to those who have experienced it.

———

The Middle Ages are often loosely referred to as "the Dark Ages." In many senses, the church of Christ did in fact become a dark place. "The lips of a priest should guard knowledge, and people should seek instruction from his mouth" (Mal. 2:7). But, as the movement within the Roman Catholic Church that we know as the Counter-Reformation was to underline, the hungry sheep were looking up but were not being fed. Stars appeared in the night sky from time to time, but dark clouds frequently obscured them. But now, as the fifteenth century dawned, behind the scenes of history, God was bringing together the factors that would be needed for a major reformation of the church to take place.

One of these factors emerging in fifteenth-century Italy was Girolamo (Jerome) Savonarola.

Girolamo Savonarola

Savonarola was born in 1452 and died in 1498. The early part of his life was spent training for a career in medicine. He became increasingly concerned about the state of society ("I could not endure any longer the wickedness of the blinded Italians," he wrote); he was also disappointed in love. Despite his personal devotion to his family, he left home and entered a Dominican monastery in Bologna. Here he studied Hebrew and Greek and developed a massive knowledge of Scripture.

Savonarola set his heart on becoming a preacher yet had little initial success. But he labored in his preaching until he found himself growing in eloquence and gaining a large hearing. Invited to Florence by Lorenzo de' Medici, he captivated the city with his preaching. A paradox often witnessed in the story of the church was reenacted in the cathedral. His fierce denunciations of sin spared no one. The people, the clergy, and even Lorenzo the Magnificent himself were regularly castigated by him from the pulpit. Yet crowds packed the cathedral on a daily basis to listen to this "force of nature" and heard such denunciations as:

> Think carefully then—you who are rich—afflictions will smite you. This city will no longer be called Florence, but a den of

thieves, of moral filth and bloodshed. Then you will all be poverty-stricken, then, you will be wretched! And your name, you priests shall be changed into an object of terror.

And then, breaking off in mid-sermon from addressing the congregation, Savonarola engages in a dramatic dialogue with God Himself:

Lord, I tried to stop speaking in your name, but you have overpowered me and conquered me. Your word has become like a fire in me. It consumes the very marrow of my bones. This is why I am derided and despised by the people. But I cry to the Lord day and night. So I say to you: There are unheard of times about to fall on you!

With such dramatic and apocalyptic preaching coming from the pulpit day after day, and a congregation whose size was increasing constantly, Savonarola continued his prophet-like assaults on the sin and ungodliness of the city. Elected prior of St. Mark's, he refused to follow the established etiquette of going to pay homage to Lorenzo the Magnificent. "I consider that my election is owed to God alone," he said, inevitably infuriating his prince.[1]

On one occasion, when Lorenzo came to hear Mass and walk in the garden of St. Mark's Convent, Savonarola simply ignored him and continued with his own study. When some of the monks came to tell him that *Il Magnifico* was present, he simply replied, "If he doesn't actually ask for me he can stay or go—whatever he wants."

Lorenzo sent him personal gifts and financial help for the monastery, which merely stimulated Savonarola to respond from the pulpit that a faithful dog does not stop barking in his master's defense simply because someone throws a bone to him. From the same pulpit, indifferent to threats of banishment, he urged some of Lorenzo's friends: "Bid him to do penance for his sins, for the Lord is not a respecter of persons. He does not spare the princes of the world!"

This was the language of a passionate reformer, a man possessed by a conviction that he spoke with the authority of a divine call. Savonarola preached, and to a certain extent managed to enforce, rigorous moral reform. In 1496, under his leadership, the city held an enormous bonfire of pornographic literature, cosmetics, and even equipment used for gambling. He had virtually become the censor of the morals of Florence, bold enough to claim that popes can err and to denounce the pope as the servant of Satan.

Savonarola also had a radical vision for the restructuring of civil life—in some senses, it was in his preaching that the modern idea of a "republic" first emerged. In effect, he promised the people of Florence a kind of "golden age" on condition of their repentance.

But eventually, Savonarola himself was accused of being a false prophet and a heretic. A "trial by fire" was to settle the issue of his faithfulness to God. One of Savonarola's friends volunteered to take his place, and preparations were made in the city square for the dramatic event. The opposing sides engaged in prolonged bickering with each other. Rain fell, sunset came, and the whole event was abandoned.

The dynamics at work behind this incident cannot now be clearly retraced. Was this all a carefully stage-managed plan to destroy Savonarola's reputation in the eyes of the people of Florence? Were there indeed daggers concealed beneath the cloaks of assassins ready to end Savonarola's life, as was rumored? In any event, the anticlimax of the occasion seemed to reduce Savonarola from a giant to an ordinary mortal in the eyes of the people.

How quickly a crowd can be swayed and turned. The pope provided the city of Florence with full absolution and financial gifts. In exchange, Savonarola and his colleagues were to be tortured and tried. Under duress, Savonarola admitted he had never been a prophet (a confession he later recanted).

Martin Luther believed that Savonarola's finest hour now came. Between tortures, he composed a series of meditations on the penitential psalms, making their petitions his own. Now—as we have seen with others—perhaps we come nearer to his heart. Here, Luther noted, we see Savonarola not as a Dominican monk and adored preacher "but as an everyday Christian."

Savonarola was pronounced excommunicate: "*Separo te ab ecclesia militante et triumphante*" (I separate you from the church militant and triumphant). "*Militante, non triumphante*" (From the militant, but not from the triumphant), replied the brave martyr, "*hoc enim tuum non est*" (for this is not within your powers). Having been forced to witness the execution of two of his friends, Savonarola was then himself executed by burning and his ashes thrown into the River Arno.

The year was 1498. Soon shock waves would flash across Europe like lightning in the night sky. Within two decades, Martin Luther would have posted his Ninety-Five Theses in Wittenberg and the Reformation would be under way.

Renaissance

Movements as well as individuals prepared the way for the Reformation. One of these movements was the Renaissance, a rebirth of interest in antiquity fed by the rediscovery of ancient texts and the development of the ability to translate them. An entire generation of able young scholars was fired with enthusiasm for the new learning, no longer content with secondhand information, repetition of traditions, or indeed with knowing only what the church had told them.

In a world dominated by Roman Catholicism, whose "authorized version" of the Bible was the Latin Vulgate (Jerome's translation), such a desire to return *ad fontes*,[2] coupled with a growing ability to read Hebrew and especially Greek, eventually led to something radically new—comparing and contrasting what the church had taught with what the New Testament actually said. In addition, the newly invented printing press now made it possible for material that formerly would have remained in manuscripts, and that would have been copied only with great labor and expense, to be published in large numbers.

Erasmus, the famous Dutch scholar, produced an edition of the Greek New Testament. Young scholars devoured it with enthusiasm. No longer did they need to read or hear the gospel secondhand but as the Apostles preached and taught it. Erasmus himself recognized that the church needed to be reformed. But even he could have had little concept as he prepared his text that his work would help to precipitate the major ecclesiastical event of the second millennium—the Protestant Reformation.

Nor did an Augustinian monk with whom that Reformation is most commonly associated.

His name?

Martin Luther.

Come Down, O Love Divine

BIANCO DA SIENA (DIED 1434)[3]

Come down, O love divine,
seek thou this soul of mine,
and visit it with thine own ardour glowing;
O Comforter, draw near,
within my heart appear,
and kindle it, thy holy flame bestowing.

O let it freely burn,
till earthly passions turn
to dust and ashes in its heat consuming;
and let thy glorious light
shine ever on my sight,
and clothe me round, the while my path illuming.

Let holy charity
mine outward vesture be,
and lowliness become mine inner clothing;
true lowliness of heart,
which takes the humbler part,
and o'er its own shortcomings weeps with loathing.

And so the yearning strong,
with which the soul will long,
shall far outpass the power of human telling;
for none can guess its grace,
till Love create a place
wherein the Holy Spirit makes a dwelling.

16

THE SIXTEENTH CENTURY
LUTHER'S DISCOVERY

After years of searching for peace with God, Martin Luther eventually experiences a breakthrough. The text below is an excerpt from his Preface to Latin Writings.

I hated that word "righteousness of God," which, according to the use and custom of all the teachers, I had been taught to understand philosophically of the formal and active justice, as they called it, by which God is righteous and punishes sinners and the unrighteous. Though I lived as a monk without reproach, I felt I was a sinner before God with a most disturbed conscience. I could not believe that he was placated by my satisfaction. I did not love, indeed I hated the righteous God who punishes sinners. Secretly, if not blasphemously, certainly murmuring greatly, I was angry with God. Yet I clung to the dear Paul and had a great yearning to know what he meant.

Finally by the mercy of God, as I meditated day and night, I paid attention to the context of the words, "In it the righteousness of God is revealed, as it is written, 'He who through faith is righteous shall live.'" Then I began to understand that the righteousness of God is that by which the righteous lives by a gift of God, namely by faith. This, then, is the meaning: the righteousness of God is revealed by the gospel, viz. the passive righteousness with which the merciful God justifies us by faith, as it is written, "The righteous one lives by faith." Here I felt that I was altogether born again and had entered paradise itself through open gates. There a totally other face of all Scripture showed itself to me. And whereas before "the righteousness of God" had filled me with hate, now it became to me inexpressibly sweet in greater love. This passage of Paul became to me a gateway to heaven. Then I ran through Scripture, as I could from memory, and I found an analogy in other terms, too, such as the work of God, i.e., what God does in us, the power of God, with which he makes us strong, the wisdom of God by which he makes us wise, the strength of God, the salvation of God, the glory of God.

———

In a number of ways, the sixteenth century, particularly in European history, marks a major watershed and signals the beginning of the modern age, characterized as it is by scientific discovery, technological advances, the movement of populations to the city, and much else.

Some of this can be traced back to the Renaissance, the rediscovery of classical texts, and learning to listen to original texts rather than to tradition-driven interpretations. This principle of returning to original texts, so important to the way in which the Reformers interpreted the book of Scripture, had a vital impact on how Christians would also learn to interpret the book of nature—no longer through the lenses of a priori philosophical assumptions but by reading it in its own light. Thus, Thomas Kepler, along with a litany of other believing scientists, saw himself as simply "thinking God's thoughts after him," and noted, "Since we astronomers are priests of the highest God in regard to the book of Nature, it befits us to be thoughtful, not of the glory of our minds, but rather, above all else, of the glory of God."

How did this pattern of reading the text of Scripture have such a revolutionary effect?

The Renaissance principle *ad fontes*, going back to the sources and examining them in their own light, had spurred on younger scholars in both linguistic and textual studies. Thus the young John Calvin's first published work was not a theological treatise but a careful and extensive linguistic commentary on a classical text, *De clementia* by Seneca the Younger (a Roman Stoic and contemporary of the Apostle Paul).

The thirteenth and fourteenth centuries witnessed the rise of various reformers such as Wycliffe, Hus, and Savonarola. As one, they had decried the corruptions of the church and its accretions to the message of the Bible, such as ignorance, immorality, and greed among the clergy. But even the Lollard movement had depended on a translation of a translation of the Bible. Now the "new learning" gave younger scholars the opportunity to compare the Greek text of the New Testament with the Latin Vulgate. At last, they could read the gospel as it was expounded by the Apostles. Now they could hear the gospel on its own terms—not secondhand through the church's tradition. The reformations called for in the previous two centuries became a call to return to the central message of the gospel itself. As the forerunners such as Wycliffe and Hus left the stage, others stepped onto it. None was more significant than the man who became the catalyst for the transformation of Europe. His name, of course, was Martin Luther.

Martin Luther

Luther was born in Saxony, northern Germany, in 1483. Raised in the relatively uneducated home of a miner, he had made his way through an undergraduate degree before he first set eyes on a Bible.

Then two dramatic events stopped him in his tracks.

The first was that one of his university friends was murdered in a brawl. As Martin thought about what had happened to his friend, he could not escape the question nagging at his conscience: What would have become of me before the judgment seat of God if I had been removed from life as suddenly as he was?

The second took place while Luther was on a journey. Suffering a leg injury in a thunderstorm, in one of the great ironic events in history, he appealed to St. Anne to intercede for his life and vowed that if he survived he would become a monk. Survive he did—and as the saying goes, the rest is history.

Before many more months had passed in 1505, Luther kept his vow and entered the Augustinian monastery at Erfurt. Two years later, he was ordained as a priest. Later, in 1511, he became a professor in the recently founded University of Wittenberg. Encouraged by his spiritual counselor, Johannes Staupitz, he proceeded to study for and gain his doctorate and was appointed professor of biblical studies in the theology faculty, a position he retained for the rest of his life.

A Troubled Conscience

Luther was a devoted monk, thought by his fellows to be a potential candidate for sainthood. In 1510, he was given the opportunity to visit Rome on behalf of the Augustinian chapter at Erfurt. Here, surely, he would find true spirituality. Instead, he saw only corruption. He returned a despondent and depressed man. He was troubled by the question, How can I be sure when I die that I am going to stand before God and be welcomed into heaven? Behind what seemed to others to be his exemplary discipline and his growing knowledge of the Bible (and in large measure because of the latter), he was increasingly concerned about his standing before God.

One biblical text that especially disturbed him was Romans 1:16–17. If the righteousness of God (*justitia Dei*) is revealed in the gospel, how could he, a sinner, escape damnation? He was far from being *homo justus*—the righteous person who could live by faith. Thus, the righteousness of God terrified rather than consoled him. Although he was a professor of theology, he came to hate Paul's words, for a righteous God would undoubtedly condemn him for his sin.

The background to Luther's thinking lay in the late-medieval *ordo salutis* (order of salvation) in which, beginning with the first reception of grace in the sacrament of baptism, the individual responded as best he could (*facere quod in se est*) with a view to infused grace eventually creating a faith suffused with love (*fides formata caritate*) on the ground of which God could righteously justify him or her—and do so "by grace."

In a nutshell, the Roman Catholic Church taught that infused grace makes us inwardly righteous so that God can justify us. But therein lay the problem. How could anyone know they had come to the point where infused grace had produced in them a perfect righteousness? This was possible only for the few "saints" who had reached great heights of holiness or had been granted a "special revelation." No wonder Cardinal Robert Bellarmine would later comment that of all Protestant heresies, assurance of salvation was the chief.

Light

As Luther continued to read and ponder these words, light dawned. He came to see that the righteousness of God that Paul had in view is not the righteousness that He demands and we lack but the righteousness that is shown in Christ to sinners, which He provides and which we receive by faith.

It was one of the great moments in the history of the church. How he loved Paul now! He had come to understand the gospel at last. Yes, God's holiness and righteousness would condemn him for his sins. He could have nothing to say in his defense before the judgment seat of God. But this righteousness—this supplied what he lacked, it gave what he could not purchase. Romans 1:16–17 spoke not of the righteousness by which God condemns us in His wrath (that is the message of Rom. 1:18–3:20) but of the righteousness of God in Jesus Christ that He gives us as a free gift. This gospel promise opened the gates of paradise for Luther, and by faith he walked in.

Ninety-Five Theses

Yet Luther was inevitably still enmeshed in the Roman church and all of its corruption.

Pope Leo X[1] was at this very time committed to completing the building project of St. Peter's in Rome. In light of the finances needed to do so, he had licensed a distribution of indulgences,[2] and these were being granted under the direction of the Dominican preacher Johannes Tetzel.

The Roman Catholic Church did not strictly speaking "sell" indulgences. The theology is altogether more sophisticated and subtle. Tetzel, however, was more straightforward (and indeed reputedly on a salary twenty times that of Professor Luther). He was able to play on the emotions of those whose parents, family, or friends were now believed to be in purgatory. Who would not seek an indulgence to relieve them of their suffering? Who would not be grateful to the Holy Father and wish to show both deep gratitude and relief in financial ways?[3] In our own day, we see the televangelists at work shamelessly telling naive and easily emotionally manipulated viewers that if finances are not forthcoming to support their ministry, many thousands who otherwise might hear the gospel and respond will go to hell. Emotional blackmail is a powerful financial lever. How much more if the people involved are one's own parents, siblings, or children?

And so, on October 31, 1517, Martin Luther, now in his mid-thirties, made his way to the Castle Church in Wittenberg and posted his Ninety-Five Theses on the church door. Originally intended as propositions for public debate, the theses were written in Latin—the language of the scholar, not of the street. Luther could have had no idea that they would echo around Europe and become the catalyst for a spiritual revolution.

Many of those who saw the papers on the Castle Church door—which seems to have served as a public notice board—would not have been able to read Latin. But soon the theses were translated into German and thereafter spread throughout Europe like wildfire—indeed, like an "act of God."

What were the Ninety-Five Theses? They were statements aimed directly at specific corruptions in the church of Luther's day, many of them related to issues of pardon, purgatory, and the power of the pope. The first of them was particularly startling:

By saying "Repent," our Lord and Master Jesus Christ willed that the whole of the life of believers should be repentance. (*Dominus et magister noster Iesus Christus dicendo "Poenitentiam agite etc." omnem vitam fidelium poenitentiam esse voluit.*)

Luther had grasped that the Vulgate translation of "Repent" (*poenitentiam agite*) was open to the misinterpretation "Do penitence (or penance)." And he had also grasped a principle that John Calvin would later expound with great clarity: penitence or repentance is not the action of a moment; it is the turning around of a life—the rejection of sin effected by the gracious work of the Holy Spirit. It cannot therefore be a single act completed in a moment; it is a style of life that lasts until glory.

Luther led a full and adventurous life that only an extensive biography can well describe. He was a remarkable man with enormous God-given energy. His speech was direct and plain and not infrequently earthy. He was a teacher of theology, a preacher of the gospel, and an author of some of the most important books in the Reformation period. Notable among his early publications was his *On the Babylonian Captivity of the Church*, which exposed the church's failures, while in *On the Freedom of a Christian* he explained how in Jesus Christ believers are set free both to love God and to serve their neighbor. Thus he wrote in a beautifully crafted sentence that captures the paradox of the gospel-centered life: "A Christian man is the most free lord of all, and subject to none; a Christian man is the most dutiful servant of all, and subject to everyone."

By his preaching, by writing, and especially by his influence in the explanation of salvation by grace through faith in Christ, Luther was used by God to transform the Christian church.

The leading Reformers in England and Scotland were influenced by his writings, often smuggled in by merchant sailors. In Scotland in particular, the martyrs of St. Andrews, Patrick Hamilton and George Wishart (whose bodyguard John Knox had been), were disciples of Luther's teaching. Likewise in England, the heroic William Tyndale left a legacy not only in his English translation of the Bible but in an entire body of literature that echoed the German Reformer's work.

Reformation *Solas*

But what did Luther teach? His chief emphases are aptly summarized in the well-known Reformation *solas*: (1) *sola Scriptura*: we come to know God through Scripture alone, not through the traditions of the church as such; (2) *sola gratia*: we come to receive forgiveness by God's grace alone, not because we are able to earn merit; (3) *sola fide*: we receive justification by faith alone, and not by faith plus something else; (4) *solus Christus*: all of God's riches are given to us in Christ alone; (5) *soli Deo gloria*: the goal of all of life is the glory of God alone.

These principles simply underlined the emphases Luther found in Scripture. But in context, what is most significant about them is not only what they stressed but what they bypassed. Neither Luther nor the other magisterial Reformers despised the church. But they saw the church as only a witness to and a powerful illustration of salvation by grace—*not* the dispenser of that salvation. In a sense, then, the church had not only failed to teach the gospel rightly; it had usurped the role of the Holy Spirit in salvation. It was the reestablishing of the Spirit's ministry in the application of redemption that brought such a sense of the immediacy of

God's grace and the joy and relief of pardon and new life in Christ. It is to Christ alone and not to the mediation of the church that we need to turn for grace and salvation.

We have not discussed here the other great Reformers—Huldrych Zwingli and Heinrich Bullinger, John Calvin and John Knox, and many others. But even this brief glance at Luther and his influence shows that the sixteenth century was a monumental period in the history of the Christian church. It was not without its faults, nor without its failures. But Christians in those days were bursting with the power and the energy of this great discovery—that the burden of their sins had been taken by Jesus Christ and they, at last, could be set free. These were days, as Knox explained, when "God gave His Holy Spirit to simple men in great abundance."

That is what we still need!

A Mighty Fortress Is Our God, a Bulwark Never Failing

MARTIN LUTHER[4]

A mighty fortress is our God, a bulwark never failing;
Our helper He, amid the flood of mortal ills prevailing:
For still our ancient foe doth seek to work us woe;
His craft and power are great, and, armed with cruel hate,
On earth is not his equal.

Did we in our own strength confide, our striving would be losing;
Were not the right Man on our side, the Man of God's own choosing:
Dost ask who that may be? Christ Jesus, it is He;
Lord Sabaoth, His Name, from age to age the same,
And He must win the battle.

And though this world, with devils filled, should threaten to undo us,
We will not fear, for God hath willed His truth to triumph through us:
The Prince of Darkness grim, we tremble not for him;
His rage we can endure, for lo, his doom is sure,
One little word shall fell him.

That word above all earthly powers, no thanks to them, abideth;
The Spirit and the gifts are ours through Him Who with us sideth:
Let goods and kindred go, this mortal life also;
The body they may kill: God's truth abideth still,
His kingdom is forever.

17

THE SEVENTEENTH CENTURY

THE PURITANS

John Bunyan's The Pilgrim's Progress, *the best-selling Christian book of all time besides the Bible, is an allegorical exploration of the Christian life. An excerpt follows.*

Then Christian began to gird up his loins, and to address himself to his journey. Then said the Interpreter, "The Comforter be always with thee, good Christian, to guide thee in the way that leads to the city."

So Christian went on his way, saying,

> Here I have seen things rare and profitable,
> Things pleasant, dreadful, things to make me stable
> In what I have begun to take in hand:
> Then let me think on them, and understand
> Wherefore they showed me were, and let me be
> Thankful, O good Interpreter, to thee.

Now I saw in my dream, that the highway up which Christian was to go was fenced on either side with a wall, and that wall was called Salvation [Isa. 26:1]. Up this way, therefore, did burdened

Christian run, but not without great difficulty, because of the load on his back.

He ran thus till he came at a place somewhat ascending; and upon that place stood a cross, and a little below, in the bottom, a sepulchre. So I saw in my dream, that just as Christian came up with the cross, his burden loosed from off his shoulders, and fell from off his back, and began to tumble, and so continued to do till it came to the mouth of the sepulchre, where it fell in, and I saw it no more.

Then was Christian glad and lightsome, and said with a merry heart, "He hath given me rest by his sorrow, and life by his death." Then he stood still a while, to look and wonder; for it was very surprising to him that the sight of the cross should thus ease him of his burden. He looked, therefore, and looked again, even till the springs that were in his head sent the waters down his cheeks [Zech. 12:10]. Now as he stood looking and weeping, behold, three Shining Ones came to him, and saluted him with, "Peace be to thee."

So the first said to him, "Thy sins be forgiven thee" [Mark 2:5]; the second stripped him of his rags, and clothed him with change of raiment [Zech. 3:4]; the third also set a mark on his forehead [Eph. 1:13] and gave him a roll with a seal upon it, which he bid him look on as he ran, and that he should give it in at the celestial gate: so they went their way. Then Christian gave three leaps for joy, and went on singing,

> Thus far did I come laden with my sin,
> Nor could aught ease the grief that I was in,
> Till I came hither. What a place is this!
> Must here be the beginning of my bliss?
> Must here the burden fall from off my back?
> Must here the strings that bound it to me crack?
> Blest cross! blest sepulchre! blest rather be
> The Man that there was put to shame for me!

———

It is impossible to understand the story of the church in the English-speaking world in the seventeenth century without taking account of the nature of the English Reformation.

It is often said—not wholly accurately—that the Reformation in England was effected by Henry VIII's marital and succession problems, whereas in Scotland it was a "people's movement." Ultimately, however, no Reformation could have taken place in either country without the work of the Spirit of God moving men and women to come to a living faith in Jesus Christ.

That said, there is no doubt that the Scottish Reformation had a more radical edge, illustrated especially by the development of the different principles governing the life of the churches in the two nations.

In Scotland, Knox had encouraged the principle that only what Scripture teaches should be mandated in the life, government, and worship of the church.[1] This was in line with the style of church life he had experienced during his exile in Frankfurt am Main, Germany, and his spell as pastor of the congregation of English-speaking refugees in Geneva. In England, by contrast, a more "Lutheran" principle prevailed: what is forbidden in Scripture should not be practiced, but much that is not specifically mandated might be permissible.

The long reign of Henry VIII (1491–1547, king from 1509) was followed in quick and radically contrasting succession by those of Edward VI (1537–53, king from 1547; his mother was Jane Seymour) and Mary Tudor (1516–58, queen from 1553; her mother was Catherine of Aragon). During these two equally brief reigns, England lurched from ongoing reformation in the church under Edward to the persecution and martyrdom of many Protestants under Mary.

On Mary's death in 1558, Elizabeth I (1533–1603; her mother was Anne Boleyn) succeeded to the throne. Throughout her long reign, she established a Protestant via media. Control over the church was retained and exercised through the hierarchy of its episcopal government.

In the nature of the case, men are not appointed bishops because they represent the most radical and reforming wing of a church. Virtually by definition, they must play a moderating role. The pyramid-like structure of episcopal government as a whole was therefore a powerful instrument in the hands of a queen committed to divine right monarchy. It readily lent itself to diffused but centralized control. Elizabeth was thus able to keep her hand on the rudder of the church as well as that of the state—albeit not without challenges from those who desired a more thorough reformation or purifying of the Church of England—hence the name *Puritan*.

Puritans

It is often true that people seem more united when they have a common opponent than when they lack one. That was, to a certain extent, true of those we know as "Puritans." They were never a completely homogenous unit. Their common desire to see the Church of England more fully reformed according to Scripture was not matched by an agreed-upon agenda or vision for what a fully reformed church might look like. Some aspired to the kind of Presbyterianism they saw in the Reformed church in Scotland; others would have been content to accept ongoing episcopacy so long as the bishops were genuine pastors and preachers. This diversity is the reason why there has been extensive discussion among historians as to how exactly to define *Puritanism*—not least because it emerged first as a pejorative term rather than as a term of self-reference.

William Perkins

One of the greatest of these early Puritan figures was William Perkins. Born in the year of Elizabeth's accession to the throne (1558) in Marston Jabbet in Warwickshire, he received his formal education at Christ's College, Cambridge (where he was a fellow until 1595). He served as lecturer (preacher) in the church of Great St. Andrews and died in 1602 at age forty-four.

Perkins has been well described as "the Puritan theologian of Tudor times."[2] He recognized the strategic significance of the pulpits of England and the central importance of Christian godliness. With this vision, he labored to proclaim the gospel. Testimony to the discipline and power of his preaching and teaching fills the three massive folio volumes of his *Works*. But more immediately, it was felt by generations of preachers in the Puritan mold. His burden was to see a genuinely biblical ministry multiplied throughout England.

Doubtless, part of the explanation for Perkins' zeal to advance the gospel lay in the fact that in his earlier days as a student at Christ's College, he had a reputation for being far from Christ. But in God's grace, like the prodigal, "he came to himself" (Luke 15:17, KJV). One day he overhead a woman threatening her son, "Hold your tongue, or I will give you to drunken Perkins yonder." Convicted of his sinfulness and drawn to faith in Christ, he laid his life before his new Master in gratitude. He began to preach, first of all to condemned prisoners in the castle jail, then for the rest of his life from the pulpit of Great St. Andrews Church in Cambridge.

Such was the impact of Perkins' ministry that when in 1602 the young John Cotton[3] heard the church bell tolling for his death, he rejoiced that his conscience would no longer be smitten by the preacher's sermons. Thomas Goodwin later recalled that when he came up to Cambridge in 1613, "the town was then filled with the discourse of the power of Mr Perkins his ministry [*sic*], still fresh in men's memories."

Perkins' preaching was marked by what is usually called the "plain style." The description is self-explanatory: it stood in sharp contrast to preaching that employed the most appealing features and techniques of classical rhetoric and oratory. In this ornate style, impression was often more important than exposition. Perkins believed preaching should conform to the Apostolic touchstone of being "the open statement of the truth" (2 Cor. 4:2). In exemplifying this biblical model, his preaching was characterized by biblical exposition delivered with "great plainness of speech" (2 Cor. 3:2, KJV). Such preaching was not lacking in rhetorical power. But it aimed at the mind, the conscience, the will, and the affections—in a word, at the "heart." Its concern was not to effect admiration of the sermon but the conversion of the hearer.

A Scottish King of England

Perkins' life almost exactly paralleled the reign of Elizabeth. In 1603, she died unmarried and childless and was succeeded by her nearest heir, James VI of Scotland (who then also became James I of England).

James had been educated in Calvinistic Scotland in the womb of its Presbyterian church. But any hopes this raised among the Puritans were soon dashed on his accession. He was committed to the theory of the "divine right of kings." He had already sought the reestablishment of episcopacy in the Scottish church. Now confronted with a number of grievances from the Puritans,[4] he announced that he would make them conform or "harry them out of the land." In due course, many of them did leave English shores, seeking refuge among the Reformed churches on the Continent as their sixteenth-century forefathers had done, and later in the New World. Famously, the *Mayflower* would set sail some five years before the death of James in 1625.

Charles I

James was succeeded by his son Charles I, during whose reign leadership in the Church of England lurched in a high Anglican, Arminian, and Catholic[5] direction, especially under William Laud, whom he appointed archbishop of Canterbury in 1630. Laud sought to impose liturgical uniformity, which Puritans viewed as an attack on their free consciences submitted to the authority of Scripture. Both Charles and his archbishop lacked what today is often described as "emotional intelligence." The "divine right of kings" theory meant more to them—at least as far as the Puritans could see—than the authority of Scripture and the crown rights of Jesus Christ over His church.

Meanwhile, the Puritans were increasingly involved and empowered in the affairs of the nation and especially in the parliamentary activities of the House of Commons. Archbishop Laud was impeached, imprisoned in the Tower of London in 1641, and then tried. He was executed on January 10, 1645. Four years later, after his defeat in the English Civil War, King Charles followed him to the scaffold on January 30, 1649.

The next day, members of Parliament gathered in St. Margaret's Church, Westminster, as they did regularly. On this occasion, they heard two sermons. The second preacher appointed for the day was the minister of the Church of St. Peter ad Vincula (St. Peter in Bonds) in Coggeshall, Essex. Parts of his sermon would later be burned by the public hangman.

Still only thirty-two years old, he was destined to become the outstanding theologian among the Puritans, and perhaps the greatest of all English theologians. He would later serve as vice-chancellor (in American terms, president) of Oxford University. His collected writings fill twenty-four large volumes. An indication of his reach and influence is found in the fact that he is probably more widely read today by Christians throughout the world than he was in his own century.

The preacher's name was John Owen (1616–83). The sermon was later published at the request of Parliament. Its text was Jeremiah 25:19–20. Its tone was measured. But part of its burden was to underline that "plausible compliances of men in authority with those against whom they are employed, are treacherous contrivances against the God of heaven, by whom they are employed."[6] In a word, monarchs are not above the law of God and are responsible to Him for the way they treat their subjects.

Owen was not alone among the Puritans in being a man of great genius. So too was Richard Baxter, who would write perhaps the most challenging book ever penned on the work of gospel ministry, *The Reformed Pastor*, as well as a library of other volumes.

After the execution of Charles and the establishment of a republic, Oliver Cromwell served as lord protector from 1653 until 1658, when, on his death, he was succeeded by his son Richard. The republican experiment in government failed, for a variety of reasons (Richard's lack of leadership gifts being one of them). Thus, in 1660, the monarchy was restored. Two years later, Puritans who would not conform (some two thousand of them) were ejected from their churches and were made subject to a series of laws calculated to break their relationships with their former congregations and to expose them to fines and imprisonment, and ultimately to break their spirits.

He Had a Dream

One minister who suffered years of privation in this way is now remembered as the most famous and perhaps greatest of all the Puritan authors. He wrote the book that, after the Bible, has been the best-selling Christian book in history. His name was John Bunyan. His book, of course, was *The Pilgrim's Progress*.

It is said that when John Owen was asked by the king what possessed him to go to listen to Bunyan preach, he responded that if he were able to preach like Bunyan he would happily sacrifice his learning. It is touching to know that the classic work of the self-educated "Bedford Tinker" was first brought into print because Owen, one of the most erudite men in the nation, recommended it to his own publisher, Nathaniel Ponder. Such was its success that the publisher was soon known as "Bunyan Ponder."

The Rise of Deism

Looking back, it is clear that, Rebekah-like, the womb of the seventeenth-century church had two "children" wrestling within it. One was the authority of Scripture; the other was the primacy of reason. For this century gave birth to both evangelical theology on the one hand and rational theology on the other. It nurtured both John Owen and Edward Herbert, the first Lord Cherbury. While the former wrote *Meditations on the Glory of Christ* and *On Communion with God the Trinity*, the latter (the older and very different brother of the great metaphysical poet George Herbert) is known as the father of English Deism. His *De Veritate*, first published in 1624, became its Bible. His writings essentially denied the need for special or saving revelation. In many ways, it became the creed of the Western world:

1. There is a God.
2. God ought to be worshiped.
3. The chief element in worship is moral virtue.
4. Repentance for sin is a universal duty.
5. There is a future life of rewards and punishments.

Bunyan's Pilgrim, who fled from the City of Destruction because of the message of the Book and sought refuge at the cross of Christ, found a grace-release from the burden on his back and strength and blessing for the journey that would lead to the Celestial City. In stark contrast, Lord Cherbury proclaimed a "gospel" without revelation, about a God without a name, for people without a church, who could compensate for their own sins and merit their own salvation. Unlike the angels, Herbert had no "good news of great joy for all people" (Luke 2:10).

Lord Cherbury's lead brought in its wake a small library of books sympathetic to his anti-supernaturalism. Their titles betray their contents: *The Reasonableness of Christianity* (1695) by John Locke (1632–1724) and *Christianity Not Mysterious* (1696) by John Toland (1670–1722). In the next century, the thesis would become plain in the title of a work by Matthew Tindal (1657–1733): *Christianity as Old as Creation* (1730). By the end of that century, Immanuel Kant had placed an exclamation point on the entire movement when he published his *Religion within the Limits of Reason Alone* (1793).

By the start of the eighteenth century, it must have seemed it was the message of Deism rather than the gospel of John Bunyan's Pilgrim that triumphed. Often scarcely veiled by Bible references, the message of Deism became the message that was heard from vast numbers of church pulpits. To many, it appeared an altogether less disturbing "gospel"— until a person really thinks through its implications. For in every age, men and women prefer to believe that salvation is within their own powers. How dare God suggest otherwise?

But God Himself gives the lie to such pretensions. For if there had been a way to bring salvation other than His Son's death on the cross, would His Father not have found it and used it? Especially when that Son cried out to Him in agony: "Father, if it is possible . . . find another way."[7]

But other way there was none. There was none in the seventeenth century, despite the confidence of Edward Herbert. There was none in the days of Peter and the Apostles: "There is salvation in no one else, for there is no other name under heaven given among men by which we must be saved" (Acts 4:12).

There is none today either.

My Song Is Love Unknown

Samuel Crossman (1624–84)

My song is love unknown,
my Saviour's love to me,
love to the loveless shown
that they might lovely be.
O who am I that for my sake
my Lord should take
frail flesh and die?

He came from his blest throne
salvation to bestow,
but men made strange, and none
the longed-for Christ would know.
But O my friend, my friend indeed,
who at my need,
his life did spend.

Sometimes they strew his way,
and his strong praises sing,
resounding all the day
hosannas to their King.
Then "Crucify!" is all their breath,
and for his death
they thirst and cry.

Why, what hath my Lord done?
What makes this rage and spite?
He made the lame to run,
he gave the blind their sight.
Sweet injuries! Yet they at these
themselves displease,
and 'gainst him rise.

They rise, and needs will have
my dear Lord made away;
a murderer they save,
the Prince of Life they slay.
Yet steadfast he to suffering goes,
that he his foes
from thence might free.

Here might I stay and sing,
no story so divine:
never was love, dear King,
never was grief like thine.
This is my friend, in whose sweet praise
I all my days
could gladly spend.

18

THE EIGHTEENTH CENTURY
REVOLUTIONS AND REVIVAL

Below are the first twenty of the seventy resolutions of the young Jonathan Edwards, penned privately in order to give his life a biblical and godly direction.

Being sensible that I am unable to do any thing without God's help, I do humbly entreat him, by his grace, to enable me to keep these Resolutions, so far as they are agreeable to his will, for Christ's sake.

Remember to read over these Resolutions once a week.

1. *Resolved*, That *I will do whatsoever* I think to be most to the glory of God, and my own good, profit, and pleasure, in the whole of my duration; without any consideration of the time, whether now, or never so many myriads of ages hence. *Resolved*, to do whatever I think to be my *duty*, and most for the good and advantage of mankind in general. *Resolved*, so to do, whatever *difficulties* I meet with, how many soever, and how great soever.

2. *Resolved*, To be continually endeavouring to find out some *new contrivance* and invention to promote the forementioned things.

3. *Resolved*, If ever I shall fall and grow dull, so as to neglect to keep any part of these Resolutions, to repent of all I can remember, when I come to myself again.

4. *Resolved*, Never *to do* any manner of thing, whether in soul or body, less or more, but what tends to the glory of God, nor *be*, nor *suffer* it, if I can possibly avoid it.

5. *Resolved*, Never to lose one moment of time, but to improve it in the most profitable way I possibly can.

6. *Resolved*, To live with all my might, while I do live.

7. *Resolved*, Never to do any thing, which I should be afraid to do if it were the last hour of my life.

8. *Resolved*, To act, in all respects, both speaking and doing, as if nobody had been so vile as I, and as if I had committed the same sins, or had the same infirmities or failings, as others; and that I will let the knowledge of their failings promote nothing but shame in myself, and prove only an occasion of my confessing my own sins and misery to God.

9. *Resolved*, To think much, on all occasions, of my dying, and of the common circumstances which attend death.

10. *Resolved*, when I feel pain, to think of the pains of martyrdom, and of hell.

11. *Resolved*, When I think of any theorem in divinity to be solved, immediately to do what I can towards solving it, if circumstances do not hinder.

12. *Resolved*, If I take delight in it as a gratification of pride, or vanity, or on any such account, immediately to throw it by.

13. *Resolved*, To be endeavouring to find out fit objects of liberality and charity.

14. *Resolved*, Never to do any thing out of revenge.

15. *Resolved*, Never to suffer the least motions of anger towards irrational beings.

16. *Resolved*, Never to speak evil of any one, so that it shall tend to his dishonour, more or less, upon no account except for some real good.

17. *Resolved*, That I will live so, as I shall wish I had done when I come to die.

18. *Resolved*, To live so, at all times, as I think is best in my most devout frames, and when I have the clearest notions of the things of the gospel, and another world.

19. *Resolved*, Never to do any thing, which I should be afraid to do, if I expected it would not be above an hour before I should hear the last trump.

20. *Resolved*, To maintain the strictest temperance in eating and drinking.

The century that opened in the year 1700 would see massive and multidimensional upheavals in the Christian West. It was a century of revolutions and revival.

The revolutions with which every schoolboy and schoolgirl was once familiar were those in industry, in the New World, and in the *Ancien Régime* in France.

Who would have imagined that by the close of the century, in the birthing process of the American Revolution, a Scottish minister and theologian would have signed the Declaration of Independence, while on the other side of the Atlantic Ocean, during the French Revolution, an actress dressed as the goddess Reason would be exalted on the high altar of Notre Dame Cathedral in Paris?

These were, of course, very differently motivated events. John Witherspoon (the Scottish minister who as president of the College of New Jersey, later to be Princeton University, signed the Declaration) believed the old Scottish doctrine that lesser magistrates could remove the greater magistrate for due cause. When someone doubted that the situation in the Colonies was "ripe" for such a revolution, he responded, "Ripe, man . . . it is rotten!" His motives, he believed, were steeped in an application of the Scriptures, which he knew intimately, and which he held that Knox, and to a lesser extent Calvin, would at least in principle have regarded as legitimate.

Enlightenment?

The French Revolution was, however, altogether differently motivated. Witherspoon believed he could, with a clear and biblically informed conscience, sign the Declaration of Independence. In stark contrast, the French Revolution, while precipitated by economic hardship and the poor financial management of the state (which had bled the country's finances in the Seven Years' War and the American Revolutionary War) was fed by an intellectual revolution that had swept through Europe during the eighteenth century. Its evangelists preached the principles—detached from God—for which the revolution stood: "liberty, equality, fraternity." It became known as the *Aufklärung*, the Enlightenment, and it marks the full flowering of the modern era.

The Enlightenment was not an organized, unified movement. The best way to think of it is to recognize that a cluster of ideas created the lenses through which the world was viewed, often without people realizing that they were viewing it through Enlightenment-crafted spectacles. From now on, man would be the measure of all things.

Nurtured in the progressive Deism of the late seventeenth century, the Enlightenment developed into a full-blown intellectual denial of the possibility of the knowledge of God. Its key figures included the Scottish polymath David Hume, who raised questions about the role of the mind in perception and critiqued the reality of miracles. Hume famously aroused Immanuel Kant from his "dogmatic slumber." In turn, Kant's own philosophical explorations of the limits of the mind led him to postulate that it cannot penetrate beyond the phenomenal realm, which refers to things that we can experience with our senses. Special revelation from God with a resultant personal knowledge of God thus became, by definition, an impossibility.

What then is left to know? Nothing except mankind and his environment. What, then, of Christianity? In essence, it is reduced to human experience without an intellectually credible transcendental foundation. To put it more plainly, theology is limited to the study of religious experience.

Kant remains an enigmatic figure. His life scarcely offers materials for a biography of any interest. He lived and taught in Königsberg (then in Prussia, now in Russia). Apparently, he did not travel more than ten miles from the place of his birth; his life was as regular as clockwork (so regular that it was said you could tell the time of day by where Kant was at that time). His influence may be hidden, but it has been profound.

We have already noticed the influence of the Enlightenment on universities where faculties of "theology" or "divinity" have gradually been renamed departments of "religious studies" (often in the school of "social sciences"). The difference might seem merely semantic, an administrative change, but it is an expression of Enlightenment thought. No longer is the subject matter the revealed *God* (whether in general or special revelation) but *man* and his religious experience. Theology has become anthropology. All religions are thus, by definition, variants of a single phenomenon. Christianity is therefore one among equals. It may be seen as *primus inter pares* (first among equals), a kind of archbishop among the bishops of the world religions. But any claim to absolute uniqueness is a priori illegitimate. Deism has triumphed. If there is a God, then we know Him only insofar as we can say something about Him from our experience. And—as the common assumption puts it—one person's experience carries as much authority and validity as another's.

Revolution and Revival

The Industrial Revolution brought radical transformation to society and was the catalyst for transforming rural into urban life and an agrarian economy into a manufacturing one.

In every age in which there is an advance in technology, changes take place in the lives of ordinary people for which they are often ill prepared. With the advances come liabilities. The Industrial Revolution brought individuals and families into the cities. Urban populations doubled rapidly, along with the attendant problems that we see again today in the rapid urbanization of the developing world.

When we stand back from these events, we are confronted with a remarkable phenomenon. Why was there a bloody revolution in France, whereas in the United Kingdom, for all the societal problems that were rife there, and for all the influence of Enlightenment thought and values, no parallel event occurred?

From a Christian point of view, part of the answer to that question is the divine one. Alexander Pope could write in true Enlightenment spirit:

Know then thyself, presume not God to scan;
The proper study of Mankind is Man. . . .
And all our Knowledge is, Ourselves to know.[1]

But another spirit was abroad both in the United Kingdom and in the American Colonies. Indeed, throughout the English-speaking world, the Spirit of God was working to bring evangelical revival and new life. To a degree, this saved England from revolution.

There is a deep mystery attached to revival. But one of its features often seems to be the way in which God prepares and brings together a number of like-minded people in prayer, commitment to holiness, and a deep burden for those who do not know Christ.

Thus, in the first half of the eighteenth century two sons of an Anglican minister, John and Charles Wesley, would come to know the son of a Gloucestershire innkeeper, George Whitefield, when all three were students at the University of Oxford and members of what became known as "the Holy Club." These young and zealous students were committed to holiness (partly under the influence of William Law's *Serious Call to a Devout and Holy Life*) and to works of charity. But they lacked a real appreciation of the grace of God in the gospel. Over a period of time, one by one they came to see the necessity of regeneration and personal faith in Christ.

Ordained as ministers in the Church of England, the Wesley brothers, Whitefield, and others encountered a deep hostility to their evangelical message. Frequently excluded from the pulpits of the parish churches, first Whitefield and then John Wesley resorted to open-air preaching, often addressing vast concourses of people. As he listened to Whitefield preaching in Philadelphia on one occasion, Benjamin Franklin carefully calculated that he was being heard by around twenty thousand people. In due course, Whitefield met and became friends with Jonathan Edwards and others in the Colonies whose ministries were being freshly empowered by the Spirit. Edwards wept the first time he heard Whitefield preach; Whitefield in turn needed the theological wisdom of Edwards in order to grow into a clearer understanding of the ways of God.

These are perhaps the names most Christians recognize and identify with the eighteenth century. But while the Wesleys' and Whitefield's spheres of labor developed beyond the Anglican Church, others focused their ministry within it.

Servants of God

John Newton (1725–1807) was one. Formerly involved in the slave trade, he had been wonderfully converted and after deep heart-searching had become an Anglican minister—one of a small minority of evangelicals in the church. Newton has long been known for his hymns, most notably "Amazing Grace." Along with the often depressive and sometimes suicidal poet William Cowper—and perhaps as a ministry to him—he composed an entire hymnbook.[2] But in his own time, he was known less for his poetry and more for his unusual wisdom. This was in fact better expressed in the letters he wrote than in the sermons he preached. Volumes of them were published, and they continue to be among the treasures of Christian literature.[3]

Newton's younger contemporary and fellow Anglican Charles Simeon (1759–1836), although often preaching throughout the British Isles, devoted his entire ministry to one particular congregation, in his case Holy Trinity in Cambridge. Here, especially in his earlier days, he faced much opposition to his expository biblical preaching. His great burden, in addition to serving his flock, was to exemplify and encourage such biblically based preaching. Thus, his own ministry became a training ground for generations of young students, many of whom served in pastoral ministry or on the mission field.

One of these was the remarkable Henry Martyn (1781–1812). An outstanding mathematics scholar at Cambridge University, Martyn was laid hold of by God, became a missionary to India in 1805, was involved in translating the New Testament into Hindustani, Arabic, and Persian, and died of tuberculosis in Tokat, Armenia, in October 1812 while en route home. His life constitutes one of the great heroic stories of the Christian church.

In a wholly different context, God was raising up William Carey (1761–1834). Carey was originally a cobbler by trade and yet a man of extraordinary intelligence and vision. From his cobbler's bench he saw the need to evangelize the world. He left England for India in 1793. Within five years, he had learned Sanskrit and translated the whole Bible into Bengali. By the end of his life, he had supervised edited translations of the Bible into thirty-six different languages and had become a catalyst for the great missionary expansion that was to characterize the nineteenth century.

What a century!

Yes, there was an Enlightenment. But the real Enlightenment has been largely overlooked by history.

I Asked the Lord That I Might Grow

John Newton

I asked the Lord that I might grow
In faith, and love, and every grace;
Might more of His salvation know,
And seek, more earnestly, His face.

'Twas He who taught me thus to pray,
And He, I trust, has answered prayer!
But it has been in such a way,
As almost drove me to despair.

I hoped that in some favored hour,
At once He'd answer my request;
And by His love's constraining pow'r,
Subdue my sins, and give me rest.

Instead of this, He made me feel
The hidden evils of my heart;
And let the angry pow'rs of hell
Assault my soul in every part.

Yea more, with His own hand He seemed
Intent to aggravate my woe;
Crossed all the fair designs I schemed,
Blasted my gourds, and laid me low.

Lord, why is this, I trembling cried,
Wilt thou pursue thy worm to death?
"'Tis in this way, the Lord replied,
I answer prayer for grace and faith.

These inward trials I employ,
From self, and pride, to set thee free;
And break thy schemes of earthly joy,
That thou may'st find thy all in Me."

19

THE NINETEENTH CENTURY

A TIME OF CONTRASTS

The sermon "The Expulsive Power of a New Affection," preached by the great Scottish theologian and visionary church leader Thomas Chalmers and excerpted below, may be the most famous sermon preached in Scotland in the nineteenth century.

> Love not the world, neither the things that are in the world. If any man love the world, the love of the Father is not in him. (1 John 2:15–17)

There are two ways in which a practical moralist may attempt to displace from the human heart its love of the world—either by a demonstration of the world's vanity, so as that the heart shall be prevailed upon simply to withdraw its regards from an object that is not worthy of it; or by setting forth another object, even God, as more worthy of its attachment. . . .

Love may be regarded in two different conditions.

The first is, when its object is at a distance, and then it becomes love in a state of desire.

The second is, when its object is in possession, and then it becomes love in a state of indulgence. . . .

Such is the grasping tendency of the human heart that it must have a something to lay hold of—and which, if wrested away without the substitution of another something in its place, would leave a void as painful to the mind as hunger is to the natural system. It may be dispossessed of one object, or of any, but it cannot be desolated of all. . . .

We know not a more sweeping interdict upon the affections of nature than that which is delivered by the apostle in the verse before us. To bid a man into whom there has not yet entered the great and ascendant influence of the principle of regeneration, to bid him withdraw his love from all the things that are in the world, is to bid him give up all the affections that are in his heart.

The world is the all of a natural man. He has not a taste nor a desire that points not to a something placed within the confines of its visible horizon. He loves nothing above it, and he cares for nothing beyond it; and to bid him love not the world, is to pass a sentence of expulsion on all the inmates of his bosom. . . . The love of the world cannot be expunged by a mere demonstration of the world's worthlessness. . . .

But may it not be supplanted by the love of that which is more worthy than itself? The heart cannot be prevailed upon to part with the world by a simple act of resignation. But may not the heart be prevailed upon to admit into its preference another, who shall subordinate the world, and bring it down from its wonted ascendency? . . . This, we trust, explains the operation of that charm which accompanies the effectual preaching of the gospel. . . . Beside the world, it places before the eye of the mind Him who made the world, and with this peculiarity, which is all its own—that in the gospel do we so behold God, as that we may love God. It is there, and there only, where God stands revealed as an object of confidence to sinners—and where our desire after Him is not chilled into apathy, by that barrier of human guilt which intercepts every approach that is not made to Him through the appointed mediator. It is the bringing in of this better hope, whereby we draw nigh unto God—and to live without hope is to live without God; and if the heart be without God, the world will then have all the ascendency. It is God apprehended by the believer as God in Christ, who alone can dispost it from this ascendency.

I n order to understand *any* century, we need to ask not only, What happened during those hundred years? but also, What seed was sown in the previous century that now came to its harvest time?

Clearly, among the most powerful seeds were those sown by the Enlightenment thinkers, such as Immanuel Kant, and the theologians who tried thereafter to pick up the pieces of religion, such as Friedrich Schleiermacher (1768–1834).

One of Kant's arguments was this: Since all of our knowledge is gained by sense experience, it is not possible for us to have immediate knowledge of anything that lies behind or beyond it. When we speak of what transcends the physical order, we can have only speculative knowledge.

In a sense, Schleiermacher took this as a starting place. Reared in the pietism of the Moravians, he inherited its emphasis on the individual, the personal, the subjective, and the experiential. It was in this tradition that Charles Wesley had taught the Methodists to sing the prayer:

O for a heart to praise my God,
A heart from sin set free
A heart that always feels thy blood,
So freely shed for me.

Here was sinless perfection and felt blood married together.

Schleiermacher published a rejoinder to the Enlightenment critics titled *On Religion: Speeches to Its Cultured Despisers* (1799). He stressed that Kant had indeed "left room for faith," and so he emphasised on the "feeling of absolute dependence" that lay at the heart of his thinking about the Christian faith. Now subjective experience was the pathway to the knowledge of God and became the principle around which Schleiermacher built his entire theological system in his major work *The Christian Faith* (1821). It is not for nothing that he became known as the father of modern theology.

One of the major questions arising in such reworked Christianity that begins with man and his experience is always: How and where does Jesus fit in to your form of Christianity? Predictably, in the case of

Enlightenment and post-Enlightenment thinking, the answer is always a form of this equation: Jesus is the One who fully and truly exhibits what we see to be the essence of Christianity.

Thus, theologically, a massive reversal took place. Christ is no longer seen as the One who comes "from above" to bring salvation and the knowledge of God to us. He is the One who emerges "from below" and shows us how to climb higher. He embodies our highest ideal for human beings. He is one with us in our relationship to God—indeed, the best of us—since He exemplifies everything we regard as the quintessence of our view of Christianity.

This is an important principle to grasp if we are to understand and critique the "Christianities" of the past two centuries. It is not a huge step from Schleiermacher to Karl Marx's notion that religion is the people's opiate (God or Jesus is essentially an easer of pain and therefore exists only to meet felt needs) and the new psychology of the twentieth century (God the Father as a projection of our own needy condition). It was said of liberal theologians' so-called quest for the historical Jesus that they were like men looking down the well of history to find Him and, when they did, the Jesus they saw there turned out to be a reflection of themselves. Thus, the twentieth century has seen every kind of Jesus from Jesus the Businessman Supreme, to Jesus the Liberator, to Jesus the Superstar, and more. The message is essentially a variation on this theme: Whatever happens to be your highest aspiration, you can have, in the words of the song recorded by Johnny Cash, "your own personal Jesus."[1] This perspective is now in the atmosphere that Christianity breathes: it is everywhere, including, sadly, in contemporary evangelicalism in which subjective experience has sometimes swallowed up objective truth.

William Wilberforce

Yet, in parallel with this theological drift, the evangelical movement of the eighteenth century gathered energy in a wide variety of ways. The story of William Wilberforce (1759–1853) is now well known. Born into a world of privilege, and briefly cared for by evangelical relatives, he threw himself into the anticipated lifestyle of an upper-class Englishman in Cambridge student society. Blessed with great natural talents, including remarkable eloquence, he became a member of Parliament while still only twenty-one. Many parliamentary seats were, for all practical purposes, "purchased," and Wilberforce spent, in 1820s money, the massive sum of £8,000 for the privilege.[2]

In 1785, encouraged by his friend Isaac Milner (brother of his former headmaster), he carefully read Philip Doddridge's famous book *The Rise and Progress of Religion in the Soul*, began to read the Bible prayerfully, and gradually was brought to a living and very decided faith in Christ as his Savior and Lord. In many ways, this was virtually a breach of etiquette in upper-class English society—so much so that Wilberforce wondered whether there could be any place for him in English public life. It was John Newton who gave him the counsel that would direct him to play the prominent role he did in the abolition of the slave trade.

The late eighteenth and early nineteenth centuries have a kind of Hebrews 11 quality to them. They abound in the narratives of heroes of the faith who would leave home, family, country, and all future earthly advancement in order to serve Christ in areas where His name was little known. The nineteenth century is the century of Mary Slessor; of Robert Moffat and his better-known son-in-law, David Livingstone; of Hudson Taylor, John Paton, and Jonathan Gosforth; and of thousands of others who lived, and in many instances died, serving their Savior in the remote parts of the earth.

The M'Cheyne Circle

One of the most remarkable of these men was William Chalmers Burns (1815–68).

In the spring of 1839, Robert Murray M'Cheyne (1813–43) was asked to join a small group of ministers on an extended trip from Scotland to the Holy Land in order to ascertain the spiritual condition of Jews throughout and beyond Europe. He left his congregation (St. Peter's, Dundee) with a sense that perhaps while he was gone God would manifest His presence in new ways. Earlier that same year, during a period of illness, he had written to a friend, "I sometimes think that a great blessing may come to my people in my absence."[3]

The twenty-four-year-old William Chalmers Burns was appointed to fill M'Cheyne's place on a temporary basis. During his absence, Burns was, under God, the means of a spiritual awakening when preaching to his father's congregation in Kilsyth. Two weeks later, delayed in returning to Dundee by the events of the revival, he shared the details with the congregation there. The same thing happened in St. Peter's. When M'Cheyne returned, he witnessed it for himself: "The night I arrived I preached to such a congregation as I never saw before," he wrote to his friend Andrew Bonar.

To those who are familiar with experiential Christianity, the names of M'Cheyne and Bonar are well known. Why is W.C. Burns' name relatively unfamiliar? He sensed that God was calling him not to continue to serve in Scotland, or indeed anywhere in the United Kingdom. In 1847, he sailed into obscurity to China, where he spent the rest of his life preaching the gospel. There he met and befriended James Hudson Taylor (1832–1905), founder of the China Inland Mission (the adjective "inland" is significant), and moved into the interior. They made a radical decision to apply Paul's principle to be "all things to all people that by all means I might save some" (1 Cor. 9:22) and adopted Chinese dress. Briefly imprisoned in Guangzhou, Burns later died unheralded in obscurity after two decades of largely hidden ministry among the Chinese people.

One wonders if contemporary Christians would have insisted that Burns stay at home where he could "do so much good." But then, perhaps, we remember China today and wonder how many of W.C. Burns' tears and prayers were stored in the divine bottle that has been "uncorked" in the massive turning to Christ that has taken place in that great nation. God's ways and thoughts are not ours. They are, indeed, much higher; they extend further. They also last much longer.

C.H. Spurgeon

No comments on the nineteenth century, however brief, should pass over the remarkable figure of Charles Haddon Spurgeon (1834–92).

Genius, visionary, controversialist, and much else, Spurgeon was a one-man minor Christian industry. While he was still in his teens, his vibrant Christ-centered preaching drew large crowds. He became pastor of a massive congregation (the Metropolitan Tabernacle, specially built for his ministry, was home to a congregation of some six thousand people). Although often plagued by illness and the low spirits that accompanied it, "C.H.S." had a zeal for God's glory, a love for Christ, and an enormous heart passion to see people come to faith, and these never grew dim.

Spurgeon's Sunday sermons were published, distributed, and widely read throughout the English-speaking world (one penny each!). His influence apparently spread far beyond people who were willing to acknowledge it—if an amusing limerick hints at the truth:

There was a young preacher called Spurgy
Who hated the Church's liturgy
But his sermons are fine,
And I use them as mine,
As do most of the Anglican clergy!

Annual volumes of his sermons continued to be published until 1917, when the shortage of paper during the First World War brought the series to a close with volume 63. He preached widely and constantly beyond his own congregation. With reputedly only one exception (which he thought disastrous), he never preached the same sermon twice. He was—among much else—also president of a theological seminary and responsible for orphanages for both boys and girls, where the practical wisdom and love of his vision seems to have combined to effect both faith and fun, and a personal and eternal sense of security for many youngsters.

Spurgeon's ministry was built on strong Calvinistic theology, immovable convictions about the inspiration and authority of Scripture, a unique ease with words, and an accompanying eloquent love for both the Savior he preached and the hearers who listened. Pathos and power characterized his preaching, a huge sense of humor made him the most attractive of friends, and at the same time a physical "thorn in the flesh" (not to mention a litany of human ones) kept him from being exalted (2 Cor. 12:7).

Among many others from the time of the Reformation onward, Spurgeon gives the lie to two false rumors. The first is that Calvinism kills evangelism. His ministry proved the contrary. The second is that evangelicalism is concerned with people's souls while liberals are concerned with their bodies. Spurgeon held to a much better biblical doctrine of God, Christ, man, the gospel, and the church. He was concerned for the salvation of people. It was because he knew they would last for all eternity in the presence of God or forever apart from it that their status before God always took priority. But he was constantly concerned about suffering and privation in their lives now.

Spurgeon died in 1892. In a sense, his death marked the end of an era in England. Within a quarter of a century, the Western world would be engulfed in the First World War (1914–18) and experience the highest loss of life since the Great Plague. But the century to come would also see a yet greater loss of church life, fueled by the yet more menacing plague of its own rejection of the gospel. So it remains now to turn the page into the final chapter of our journey through the Christian centuries.

Here, O My Lord, I See Thee Face to Face

HORATIUS BONAR

Here, O my Lord, I see Thee face to face;
Here would I touch and handle things unseen;
Here grasp with firmer hand the eternal grace,
And all my weariness upon Thee lean.

This is the hour of banquet and of song;
This is the heavenly table spread for me;
Here let me feast, and feasting, still prolong
The hallowed hour of fellowship with Thee.

Here would I feed upon the bread of God,
Here drink with Thee the royal wine of heaven;
Here would I lay aside each earthly load,
Here taste afresh the calm of sin forgiven.

I have no help but thine; nor do I need
Another arm save thine to lean upon;
It is enough, my Lord, enough indeed;
My strength is in thy might, thy might alone.

Mine is the sin, but thine the righteousness:
Mine is the guilt, but thine the cleansing blood
Here is my robe, my refuge, and my peace;
Thy Blood, thy righteousness, O Lord my God!

Too soon we rise; the symbols disappear;
The feast, though not the love, is past and gone.
The bread and wine remove; but Thou art here,
Nearer than ever, still my shield and sun.

Feast after feast thus comes and passes by;
Yet, passing, points to the glad feast above,
Giving sweet foretaste of the festal joy,
The Lamb's great bridal feast of bliss and love.

20

THE TWENTIETH CENTURY

HOPE

Dietrich Bonhoeffer's exposition of the Christian life emphasizes the costliness of grace. The text below is excerpted from The Cost of Discipleship.

Cheap grace means grace sold on the market like cheapjacks' wares. The sacraments, the forgiveness of sin, and the consolations of religion are thrown away at cut prices. Grace is represented as the Church's inexhaustible treasury, from which she showers blessings with generous hands, without asking questions or fixing limits. Grace without price; grace without cost! The essence of grace, we suppose, is that the account has been paid in advance; and, because it has been paid, everything can be had for nothing. Since the cost was infinite, the possibilities of using and spending it are infinite. What would grace be if it were not cheap? . . .

Cheap grace is the preaching of forgiveness without requiring repentance, baptism without church discipline, Communion without confession, absolution without personal confession. Cheap grace is grace without discipleship, grace without the cross, grace without Jesus Christ, living and incarnate.

Costly grace is the treasure hidden in the field; for the sake of it a man will go and sell all that he has. It is the pearl of great price to buy which the merchant will sell all his goods. It is the kingly rule of Christ, for whose sake a man will pluck out the eye which causes him to stumble; it is the call of Jesus Christ at which the disciple leaves his nets and follows him.

Costly grace is the gospel which must be *sought* again and again, the gift which must be *asked* for, the door at which a man must *knock*.

Such grace is *costly* because it calls us to follow, and it is *grace* because it calls us to follow *Jesus Christ*. It is costly because it costs a man his life, and it is grace because it gives a man the only true life. It is costly because it condemns sin, and grace because it justifies the sinner. Above all, it is *costly* because it cost God the life of his Son: "ye were bought at a price," and what has cost God much cannot be cheap for us. Above all, it is *grace* because God did not reckon his Son too dear a price to pay for our life, but delivered him up for us. Costly grace is the Incarnation of God.

———

S tanding, as we do, in the twenty-first century, and in the English-speaking world, it might seem that in many places in the world the church of Christ is on its last legs. This is simultaneously a cause for rejoicing among its opponents and a great grief to Christian people. Only the spiritually blind or falsely triumphalist can be pain free. Yet two considerations preserve Christians from pessimism. The first is the word of Christ that stands as the undergirding theme of these pages. He has promised to build His church; He has also promised that not even the powerful gates of Hades will overcome it. And, in addition, before our very eyes, as it were, He has brought more people to living faith than at any other time in all previous Christian centuries.

What a century! True, already in the eighteenth century, Jonathan Edwards believed that a time would come when people would be able to move across the face of the earth at speeds inconceivable in his day. But who could have envisaged the technological capability, and the instantaneous contact with any part of the world, that would become universally available and affordable? John Calvin, John Owen, and Jonathan Edwards could hardly have imagined that their massive collected works could be carried around in a format that fits into a pocket, far less that more people would read their writings today than at any time since they were written.

The twentieth century was indeed an amazing century. Plus we know much more about it than any other period in history. But perhaps we are much too close to it, and know so relatively little of the influences flowing from it that will dominate the shape of the future, to be able to choose the moments or individuals of greatest significance in it.

Optimism Destroyed

The twentieth century opened confidently enough for the Christian church. In 1910, a major missionary conference took place in Edinburgh, Scotland. In his closing address, the chairman, Dr. John Mott, ended in oft-quoted words by calling for "the evangelization of the world in our time" and predicting that the end of the conference might mark the beginning of the conquest.

Almost from that utterance, we can mark the decline of the profess-ing Christian church in the Western world.

Two World Wars, the Holocaust, the rise and fall of communism, conflict in the Middle East, genocide in many countries, and the radical transformation of the moral norms of the West in the second half of the century are all part of the story that shapes the psyche of our generation.

For some, the most appropriate summary of the role of the Christian church in these decades would doubtless be a despairing "Ichabod"— where is the glory? After all, Western Christianity appears to be heading into the night.

The century began with the collapse of the optimism that had char-acterized liberal theology's confidence. In Richard Niebuhr's famous words, it proclaimed, "A God without wrath brought men without sin into a kingdom without judgment through the ministrations of a Christ without a cross."[1] Yet its substitution by Neoorthodoxy brought no life to churches. The ongoing drift toward theological dilution, pluralism, and various forms of syncretism in the mainstream churches in the West is now bringing about at least the appearance of terminal decline. Lead-ers in the churches now openly deny the inspiration and authority of Scripture, along with its cardinal doctrines and lifestyle directives. The declining number of individuals entering the ministry of these churches only serves to highlight a loss of any sense of the thrilling and all-demanding task of preaching the gospel, pastoring the people of God, and reaching the world for Christ. Meanwhile, leaders naively continue to report that "the church is in good heart," and in some instances arro-gantly demean the conservatism of the growing churches of the Global South.

Should we "lose heart"? Surely not any more than the Apostle Paul was prepared to do (2 Cor. 4:1, 16; 5:6). For faith in the promises of God always brings hope; Christ will build His church. Not only so, but He has given as powerful illustrations of His church-building in the twenti-eth century as in any century that preceded it.

In China, 1900 was the year of the so-called Boxer Rebellion and inaugurated a season in which numbers of Christians, both Chinese and missionaries from other parts of the world, laid down their lives for Jesus Christ. Later in the century, the destruction of the church seemed to be guaranteed by the Cultural Revolution under the leadership of Chairman Mao Zedong (1893–1976). The almost ubiquitous presence of the little red book of the *Thoughts of Chairman Mao* even in the West seemed to mark the end of the Bible as the world's best-selling book.

And yet, as we look back on the twentieth century, need we lose heart? Certainly not, for two reasons.

Hope

The first is because Christ has promised that the gates of hell will never prevail against His church.

The second is that despite the decline of the church in the West and the rise of militant Islam (often masking the very large numbers of people in the Islamic world who have become Christian believers), the number of Christians in the world has dramatically increased. Had we the ability to see the real spiritual situation, we would perhaps conclude that Jesus Christ has never been more active than He is today in building the church in the power of the Spirit through the message of the gospel.

There are far more Christians in the world today than at any time in all the previous centuries. It is also true that there appear to have been more people martyred as professing Christians in the twentieth century than perhaps in all other centuries put together. But if we recall Tertullian's famous words in the second century that "the blood of martyrs is seed," we will understand that in the economy of heaven, these two things are not unrelated. As death works in believers, Christ works life in unbelievers (see 2 Cor. 4:10–12). "The government of the Church of Christ has been so constituted from the beginning," Calvin wrote, "that the Cross has been the way to victory, death the way to life."[2]

When, if ever, did you last see a copy of Chairman Mao's little red book? By contrast, the best guesses at the number of Christian believers in China today provide staggering statistics. So much so that in April 2014, staff of the quality British secular newspaper *The Telegraph* reported that within the next decade or so, China may become "the world's most Christian nation."[3]

Did any of the missionaries who were driven out of China at the time of the Boxer Rebellion or the relatively small number of Christians in the days of the Cultural Revolution dream in faith that by the close of the first quarter of the next century there might be more evangelical Christians in the nation of China than in any other country in the world? What is the explanation? There is only one—Jesus Christ has been building His church and answering the prayers of His people who have never stopped believing His promise.

The Book of the Century?

Any thinking Christian, reflecting on the twenty centuries of Christian faith that now lie in the past, might turn to his or her library to gaze at the Christian books that tell the story of the church's faith and life.

Is there a book that might capture the story of the twentieth century?

One possibility is the English translation of the famous commentary on Romans (*Der Römerbrief*) by the Swiss theologian Karl Barth (1886–1968). Published in 1919, it fell, as one commentator said, "like a bomb on the theologians' playground" and was the harbinger of a seismic Neoorthodox shift in Western theology. Is this—or the many other books to which Neoorthodoxy gave birth—the volume that epitomizes the church in the twentieth century? Or should we turn to the theological works of Rudolph Bultmann (1884–1976) or the *Systematic Theology* of Paul Tillich (1886–1965) or the liberation theology of Gustavo Guitiérrez (b. 1928) or the powerful writing of Jürgen Moltmann (b. 1926)?

At the other end of the theological spectrum is the enormously influential book of J.I. Packer (b. 1926) titled *Knowing God*, the sales of which served as an index of the resurgence of Reformed theology, which has been such a worldwide phenomenon in the twentieth century. Is this the book that best gives us the flavor of what Christ has been doing?

Perhaps there is a book one could select and about which one could say, "Here is the story." It is not a narrative, nor a work of theology, but a book of statistics: *Operation World*, begun by Patrick Johnstone. At first glance, it might seem intensely boring. But its superabundance of statistics tells us that throughout the world there are millions of boys and girls, young people, men and women, some of them in the most unlikely places, some facing enormous personal pressure and persecution, who follow Jesus Christ and are the living proof of His promise, "I will build my church; and the gates of hell shall not prevail against it."

Two Thousand Years of Christianity

Two thousand years ago, around the year AD 30, the Lord Jesus stood with His eleven remaining Apostles whom a few years previously He had called to be with Him. Now He was sending them out into the world. He said:

> Go therefore and make disciples of all nations, baptizing them in the name of the Father and of the Son and of the Holy Spirit, teaching them to observe all that I have commanded you. And behold, I am with you always, to the end of the age. (Matt. 28:18–20)

Eighteen hundred years later, David Livingstone (1813–73) wrote in his journal:

> I read that Jesus came and said, "All power is given unto me in heaven and in earth. Go ye therefore, and teach all nations—and lo, I am with you always, even unto the end of the world." It is the word of a Gentleman of the most sacred and strictest honour, so there's an end of it.

In 1858, Livingstone received the honorary doctor of laws degree at the University of Glasgow. Few sights could have been more awe-inspiring to the young graduates in their late teens and early twenties privileged to witness the scene. Here was a Christian man, like some of them born in the most modest of homes. We can almost see him in our mind's eye as he rises to address them. His left arm hangs limp as the result of an attack by a lion;

his body is obviously weakened by almost constant attacks of tropical fever. But listen to him telling these young men that he would return to Africa:

> I return without misgiving and with gladness of heart. For would you like me to tell you what supported me through all the years of exile among people whose attitude toward me was always uncertain and often hostile? It was this: "Lo, I am with you always, even unto the end of the world." On those words I staked everything and they never failed! I was never left alone.

A vast army of men and women, young people, and boys and girls bear witness in every century to the fact that Jesus Christ has kept this promise. He is still building His church. He is still with His people. He will be with them until the end of the world, and then forever.

This is the ongoing story of *In the Year of Our Lord*.

Saints of Zion

R.C. Sproul[4]

From Abel's favor'd off'ring to Jesus' holy cross,
The church of God's own choosing has triumphed over loss.
Then come, O saints of Zion in sweet communion wed;
The bride awaits her glory: Lord Jesus Christ her head.

By faith our fathers labored; in faith they lived and died.
From Abraham to David, faith stood when it was tried.
Then come, O saints of Zion in sweet communion wed;
The bride awaits her glory: Lord Jesus Christ her head.

This covenant of grace divine, by Christ's own blood was bought;
The promises of blessing shall never come to nought.
Then come, O saints of Zion in sweet communion wed;
The bride awaits her glory: Lord Jesus Christ her head.

By martyr's death the holy seed was sown in grief and pain,
That holy seed will flourish till Christ shall come again.
Then come, O saints of Zion in sweet communion wed;
The bride awaits her glory: Lord Jesus Christ her head.

The church of God triumphant shall in that final day
Have all her sons and daughters home from the well fraught fray.
Then come, O saints of Zion in sweet communion wed;
The bride awaits her glory: Lord Jesus Christ her head.

NOTES

Introduction

1 William Knight, *Colloquia Peripatetica: Notes of Conversations with the late John Duncan, LL.D.* (Edinburgh, Scotland: David Douglas, 1879), 9. The reference is to John Owen (1616–83), the greatest of the English Puritan theologians.

2 *"Just a Talker": Sayings of John ("Rabbi") Duncan*, ed. J.M. Brentnall (Edinburgh, Scotland: Banner of Truth, 1997), 181.

3 An edited version of the original talks was published as *Church History 101: Highlights of Twenty Centuries*, coauthored with Joel R. Beeke and Michael A.G. Haykin (Grand Rapids, Mich.: Reformation Heritage, 2016), and also in *The Reformation Heritage KJV Study Bible*, eds. J.R. Beeke, M.P.V. Barrett, G.M. Bilkes, and P.M. Smalley (Grand Rapids, Mich.: Reformation Heritage, 2014), 1941–62.

Chapter 1

1 In his Gifford lectures at the University of Edinburgh, given in 1927–28 and later published. A.N. Whitehead, *Process and Reality* (originally published in 1929), corrected ed., eds. D.R. Griffin and D.W. Sherburne (New York: The Free Press, 1979), 39.

2 The narrative is found in all three Synoptic Gospels: Matthew 4:1–11; Mark 1:12–13; Luke 4:1–13.

3 Revelation 1:9. Patmos is one of the (Greek) Dodecanese Islands off the coast of Miletus in modern-day Turkey.

4 *Apology* (Greek *apologia*, "defense").

5 Tertullian, *Ad nationes,* xvii. A decury is a company of ten men (from the Latin *decem,* "ten").

6 *Apology,* chapter 50.

Chapter 2

1 Tertullian, *Ad nationes,* 1:viii.

2 Titus Flavius Domitian (51–96; reigned 81–96).

3 Atheism in the Hellenistic world did not mean not believing in the existence of God (as today) but not believing in the traditional gods. Famously, Plato records how Socrates was condemned to death (by drinking hemlock) for impiety because he failed to acknowledge the gods the city (Athens) did and introduced new gods.

4 Domitilla was the daughter of the emperor Vespasian.

5 Ignatius (c. 35–c. 107) is known to us through the letters he wrote to various early Christian churches while en route to his martyrdom in Rome.

6   Polycarp (c. 69–155), bishop of the church in Smyrna (modern-day Izmir, Turkey), serves as a remarkable link between Ignatius and the great early theologian Irenaeus of Lyons (c.130–c. 200), who heard him preach when he himself was a boy.

7   This lies behind Paul's words in 1 Corinthians 8:5.

8   The heresy known as Docetism (from the Greek verb *dokeō*, to seem).

9   This way of thinking permeates the letter to the Hebrews, for example in 2:10–11, 14, 17–18.

10 The shrewd and telling title of a book by C. FitzSimmons Allison (Harrisburg, Pa.: Morehouse, 1994).

Chapter 3

1   Not to be confused with the earlier and more famous First Council of Constantinople in 381. The synod in 543, under the direction of the emperor Justinian, published a series of nine anathemas directed against Origen's teaching. These had earlier formed a conclusion to Justinian's work *Adversus Origenem liber* (Book against Origen).

2   See Paul's devastating words in 2 Corinthians 10:12.

3   Notably, at the incarnation, baptism, death, and resurrection of Jesus.

4   Translated by George Ratcliffe Woodward (1910, alt.).

Chapter 4

1   The title of a book by Arnold Lunn and Garth Lean (London: Blandford, 1965).

2   The phrase is taken from a poem by Amy Carmichael, *Gold Cord, The Story of a Fellowship* (London: SPCK, 1952), x.

3   From the Greek word for desert (*erēmos*).

4   Lactantius (c. 240–c. 320), a convert to Christianity, was a tutor in the household of Constantine and an author.

5   October 28, 312.

6   Born sometime between 260 and 280, he died in 326.

7   C. 296–373.

8   Augustine, *Confessions*, V.xiii (23), trans. Henry Chadwick (Oxford, England: Oxford University Press, 1991), 88; emphasis added.

9   Translated from Martin Luther's German edition by William M. Reynolds.

Chapter 5

1   In this context, it is significant that what Augustine's teaching undermines is not human responsibility but human pride and self-sufficiency.

2   Augustine, *Confessions*, 202.

3   *Concerning the Corruption of Sin and Grace*, 12:33. His *Enchiridion* (chapter 118) expounds these four stages. They would make a reappearance in, e.g., the Westminster Confession of Faith, chapter 9, "Of Free Will" (1647), and famously in Thomas Boston's great book *Human Nature in Its Fourfold State* (1720).

4   At a synod in Carthage in 418 when a series of anti-Pelagian canons was published.

5   This may have been in the region of Hadrian's Wall that ran from the Solway Firth in the

west to the River Tyne in the east. Other claims for a birthplace include Gaul, Scotland, Wales, and, of course, Ireland.

Chapter 6

1 Publius Cornelius Tacitus, *Life of Gnaeus Julius Agricola,* chapter 10.
2 It may also help some readers if it is remembered that Celtic Catholicism did not regard itself as identical with Roman Catholicism.
3 Contrast this with the unwise comment made by at least one Christian "leader" that the 2004 movie *The Passion of the Christ* was the greatest evangelistic tool in modern history (greater than the church Jesus Himself has been building for two thousand years?).
4 Amusing as it may seem, the use of "you" and "y'all" in a translation would enable the reader immediately to grasp the force of any given statement in the New Testament.
5 At Durrow and Derry.
6 He was held to be partly responsible for the Battle of Cúl-drebene in 561.
7 Kentigern died in 612. Brought up in the monastic school at Culross, he founded the church in Glasgow and is reputed also to have been the teacher of Asaph at Llanelwy, Wales (later St. Asaph).
8 Nicholas Lasch, *The Cult of Narcissism* (New York: Norton, 1979).
9 Translated from the Latin by Duncan MacGregor.

Chapter 7

1 *The Koran,* trans. George Sale (London: Frederick Warne, n.d.), 94 (IV.6): "He was represented *by one* in his likeness."
2 Translated by John M. Neale (1818–66).

Chapter 8

1 In the Eastern church, the view developed that the entire world is "sacramental." But if everything is "sacramental," it is difficult to see any special significance in the sacraments.
2 Now part of Devon in southwest England.
3 Thor was basically the northern European equivalent of "Jove." Curiously, reverence for him finds its most lasting symbol in the name of the fifth day of the week (Thor's-Day). Even the Christianization process did not manage to erase paganism root and branch, a constant reminder to believers that Christ is building His church on enemy-occupied territory: we live the Christian life during days of the weeks that have been named in dedication to pagan gods!
4 Luke 19:40.
5 It is more than nine feet (2.79 m) high, is made of black limestone, and is today preserved in the Forest of Stelae in Xian.
6 Translated by John Mason Neale (1862).

Chapter 9

1 "Pseudo" because false. Their authenticity was being questioned already in the ninth century.
2 Gottschalk did, however, go further than Augustine in terms of the way he explored preterition (the divine "passing by" of sinners) and reprobation.

3   Translated by John Mason Neale (1862).

Chapter 10

1   Arnulf's words were apparently taken down by Gerbert d'Aurillac and expressed in this form. Gerbert himself later became pope (as Sylvester II).
2   The reference is to 2 Thessalonians 2:4.
3   In a letter to Bishop Mandell Creighton, which was part of an extended correspondence between Acton and Creighton in the context of the former's review of the latter's multivolume *History of the Papacy*. Part of the correspondence is printed as an appendix to a collection of Acton's writings, *Historical Essays and Studies*, eds. J.N. Figgis and R.V. Laurence (London: Macmillan, 1907), 504.
4   Incredible though it may seem to some readers, there are now such people as "ministry monetizing mentors" who, to quote from the website of one, work "exclusively with Christian ministry leaders, authors, speakers and coaches to create a detailed and focused plan, designed specifically to increase their individual impact and income."
5   Stephen II was pope for only three days, and thereafter the enumeration of Stephens sometimes takes account of him and at other times ignores him. *The Catholic Encyclopedia* lists this pope as Stephen VI (VII).
6   Translated by John Mason Neale.

Chapter 11

1   In the Christological controversy settled at Nicaea, Athanasius had contended against Arius that Christ is *homoousios* (of the same substance) with the Father, not, as Arius claimed, *homoiousios* (of like substance). One letter made all the difference between Christ's being fully God and His being less fully, truly, and self-sufficiently divine than the Father.
2   The pallium is the white Y-shaped vestment worn by the pope and bestowed on archbishops and metropolitan bishops as a symbol of their participation in his authority.
3   *Proslogion*, chapter 2.
4   Anselm's contemporary Gaunilo, a Benedictine monk at Marmoutier Abbey near Tours, argued against this form of reasoning by way of analogy: the fact that one can have the concept of a perfect island does not prove that such an island actually exists.
5   Theology expressing what is known from general revelation in the nature of the created order.
6   Herman Bavinck, *Reformed Dogmatics*, vol. 2, *God and Creation*, ed. John Bolt, trans. John Vriend (Grand Rapids, Mich.: Baker, 2004), 78.
7   Sermon 43.7.9.
8   As the great seventeenth-century scientist Johannes Kepler put it, "I am thinking thy thoughts after thee." *The Harmonies of the World*, book V.
9   In one sense, C.S. Lewis' best-selling *The Lion, the Witch, and the Wardrobe* accomplishes something similar for many people, so much so that one sometimes hears people say that Aslan (the lion hero of the narrative) *is* Jesus. But, of course, the book operates precisely on Anselm's *remoto Christo* principle. What Lewis does is to describe how the logic of the Christian gospel works in the fictional world of Narnia.

10 *Cur Deus homo*, chapter 21.

11 Although this theme cannot be developed here, the fact that the New Testament describes Christ's work in terms of substitution, expiation, propitiation, reconciliation, justification, victory, etc., indicates that the sin for which He atones and from which He redeems and delivers us must also be multivalent.

12 Sadly, in the Crusades, plenary indulgences were on offer to all who participated; eternal life was promised to any who lost their lives.

13 Translated by John David Chambers (1803–93).

Chapter 12

1 Published by Innocent IV. Titles of papal bulls (from the Latin *bulla*, the lead seal used to authenticate a formal document) or encyclicals are drawn from the opening words of the document.

2 While the contemporary Roman Catholic Church defends as biblical the principle that lay behind the work of the Inquisition (interpreted essentially as defending the orthodox faith and the life of the church), it has issued statements describing the work of individual inquisitors as "regrettable" and contrary to "the legitimate rights of the human person." In Roman Catholic historical apologetics, two tendencies are evident: (1) a tendency to minimize as far as possible the actual numbers of those persecuted, and (2) an even stronger tendency to distance the activity of individuals from the position and activity of the church as a whole (since it is always "holy"). This said, *the* theologian of the church, Thomas Aquinas, defended the practice (*Summa Theologica* II.II.11: Article 3: Of Heresy). In 1233, Gregory IX took the work of the Inquisition out of the hands of the bishops and made it the province of the Dominican Order, which was not answerable to the bishops. Paradoxically, it later became the province of the Franciscans, the order founded by Francis of Assisi.

3 Alexander (1186–1245) was an English Franciscan theologian who taught at the University of Paris. He became known as *Doctor Irrefragabilis* (the Irrefutable Doctor of the church).

4 Abelard had already established his reputation for being "difficult" by criticizing the "Realism" of his own teacher William of Champeaux. Realism (in this scholastic context) is the view that concepts (universals) have an existence independent of their specific embodiment (particulars). The debate between Realism and Nominalism (the view that universals are simply humanly devised concepts and have no existence apart from their specific embodiment) undergirds much medieval scholastic philosophy and theology.

5 *Sic et non*, question 85. Abelard cites both Jerome and Bede to provide the answer. Jerome (345–420) had set the benchmark for this discussion: "During the fourth watch of the night, the Lord, walking on the sea, came to the disciples. So also he was born during the fourth watch of the night, on the eighth day before the kalends of January; and rose from the dead during the fourth watch of the night, on the sixth day before the kalends of April; and will come for the Judgment during the fourth watch of the night." The Venerable Bede (c. 675–735) was a little more venerable and modest in his

exposition: "The Lord rose at the end of the night." See Priscilla Troop, *Yes and No: The Complete English Translation of Peter Abelard's Sic et Non*, 2nd ed. (Charlotte, Vt.: MedievalMS, 2008), 212.

6 *Colloquia* III.152.

7 Bernard was instrumental in the condemnation of Abelard at the Council of Sens in 1140.

8 Lombardy in northern Italy.

9 For example, he shared Abelard's view of the atonement (*Sentences* 3.19).

10 Thomas Aquinas, John Duns Scotus, and many others left commentaries on the *Sentences*. Martin Luther left marginal notes on them. Remarkably, there are about thirty commentaries on the *Sentences* available in digital form online.

11 The sword that issues from the mouth of Christ is the Word of God (Rev. 19:15).

12 Translated by Ray Palmer.

Chapter 13

1 Ugolino was a nephew of Pope Innocent III and was himself elected pope in 1227 at the age of eighty, taking the name Gregory IX. His "accomplishments" included confiscating copies of the Jewish Talmud and suspending and then excommunicating the Roman emperor Frederick II for failing to promote the Sixth Crusade. His enemies viewed him as the Antichrist (an indication, incidentally, that this idea arose first of all within the Roman Catholic Church itself, not from the Protestant Reformers). He appointed the Dominicans as official inquisitors.

2 Albertus was born around 1200 and died in 1280. Enormously learned, he was an expert on the thought of Aristotle, whose works had only recently been rediscovered in the West.

3 In connection with the work, Thomas comments, "I have set myself the task of making known, as far as my limited powers will allow, the truth that the Catholic faith professes, and setting aside the errors that are opposed to it" (*Summa Contra Gentiles*, trans. A.C. Pegis [Notre Dame, Ind.: University of Notre Dame Press, 1975], book one: God, 62 [1.2.2]).

4 In his (surprisingly) brief discussion, Thomas lists five ways in which he holds existence of God can be proved. *Summa Theologiae*, I, qu. 2, article 3.

5 *Cur Deus homo*, chapter XXI.

6 Perhaps the most famous story of Thomas records the pope showing him the treasures of the Vatican and saying "So you see, Thomas, the successor of Peter need no longer say 'Silver and gold have I none'!" To this Thomas allegedly replied, "And neither can he say 'In the name of Jesus Christ of Nazareth, rise up and walk'!"

Chapter 14

1 His name is found in a variety of spellings. It should be remembered that before the days of printing and dictionaries (and even for a time thereafter) neither words nor names enjoyed "fixed" spelling. Wycliffe's name (like Shakespeare's) exists in at least a dozen different spellings.

2   He regarded the so-called Donation of Constantine (the forged decree transferring authority over the Western Roman Empire to the pope) as a disaster for the church's spirituality.

3   Over the past century, historians have disputed the tradition that Wycliffe himself translated the Vulgate (Latin) Bible into English. In a sense, the issue is secondary. Yet the tradition that he did goes back to within two decades of his death. Whether in person or by his inspiration, the work was certainly rooted in his life and testimony.

4   Hence the significance of the name of the missionary society known as Wycliffe Bible Translators. Still today, according to this group, only about 10 percent of the world's languages have the complete translated Bible.

5   The purchasing of clerical offices and their financial benefits—so called after Simon Magus (Acts 8:18–24).

Chapter 15

1   Lorenzo de' Medici or *Il Magnifico* (1449–92) was the patron of Botticelli and Michelangelo and the de facto ruler of Florence.

2   To the fountains, i.e., the original sources.

3   Translated by Richard Frederick Littledale Jr. (1867).

Chapter 16

1   Leo X was born Giovanni di Lorenzo de' Medici and was the second son of Lorenzo *Il Magnifico*.

2   Granted by the pope, an indulgence remitted all or part of the debt of temporal punishment a sinner owed, allowing the individual to access the treasury of the (supererogatory) merits of the saints for himself or for others.

3   The theological language describing the transactions involved in receiving an indulgence was more carefully crafted than the crass ways in which they were offered on the street.

4   Translated by Frederic H. Hedge (1805–90). It is one of the ironies of the history of hymnology that the best-known hymn of the vigorously Trinitarian Reformer Martin Luther should have been translated by a leading nineteenth-century Unitarian minister. Hedge was a fellow student at Harvard Divinity School with Ralph Waldo Emerson and a founder of the Transcendentalist Club (which at one time was known as "Hedge's Club," although he later distanced himself from it).

Chapter 17

1   This is the so-called Puritan Principle expressed in the Westminster Confession of Faith (1647) that what is mandated in the church must be explicitly mandated in Scripture or deduced from it by good and necessary consequence (WCF 1.6).

2   M.M. Knappen, *Tudor Puritanism* (Chicago: University of Chicago Press, 1939), 375.

3   John Cotton later became minister in Boston, Lincolnshire, and thereafter in Boston, Mass., and through his ministry and writings was one of the most influential of seventeenth-century Puritans in both old and new England.

4   The quaintly named Millenary Petition was presented to him while he was en route to London in 1603. It contained a list of requests for church reformation and was said to

have contained the signatures of a thousand Puritan-minded ministers (hence "mille-nary," from the Latin *mille*, "thousand").

5 Charles' wife, Henrietta Maria (1609–66), daughter of Henry IV of France, was a Roman Catholic.

6 *The Works of John Owen*, ed. W.H. Goold (Edinburgh, Scotland: Johnstone & Hunter, 1850–53), 8:144.

7 See Mark 14:33–36; Luke 22:41–44.

Chapter 18

1 Alexander Pope, *Essay on Man.*

2 *The Olney Hymnbook*, named after the parish where Newton was minister.

3 See *The Works of John Newton*, 4 vols. (Edinburgh, Scotland: Banner of Truth Trust, 2015).

Chapter 19

1 "Personal Jesus" from *American IV: The Man Comes Around.* It should be said that for Johnny Cash the meaning of the song was a great deal more evangelical than its original writer (Martin Gore of Depeche Mode) intended.

2 There are various formulae used to assess the value of a sum of money in twenty-first-century terms, but a conservative estimate here would be that Wilberforce's outlay was around one million dollars.

3 In a letter written in January 1839. A.A. Bonar, *Memoir and Remains of R.M. M'Cheyne* (1892; repr., Edinburgh, Scotland: Banner of Truth, 1966), 85.

Chapter 20

1 Richard Niebuhr, *The Kingdom of God in America* (New York: Harper and Row [1937], 1959), 193.

2 John Calvin, *The Epistle of Paul the Apostle to the Hebrews and 1st and 2nd Epistles of Peter*, eds. David W. Torrance and Thomas F. Torrance, trans. W.B. Johnston (Edinburgh, Scotland: Oliver and Boyd, 1963), 240.

3 Tom Phillips, "China on course to become 'world's most Christian nation' within 15 years," *The Telegraph*, April 19, 2014, http://www.telegraph.co.uk/news/worldnews/asia/china/10776023/China-on-course-to-become-worlds-most-Christian-nation-within-15-years.html.

4 Written for the bicentenary of First Presbyterian Church, Columbia, S.C.

INDEX

ABOUT THE AUTHOR

Dr. Sinclair B. Ferguson is a Ligonier Ministries teaching fellow, Chancellor's Professor of Systematic Theology at Reformed Theological Seminary, and the evening preacher at St. Peter's Free Church in Dundee, Scotland. He previously served as senior minister of the historic First Presbyterian Church in Columbia, S.C.

A graduate of the University of Aberdeen, Scotland, Dr. Ferguson is author of some fifty books, including *The Whole Christ, Devoted to God, In Christ Alone: Living the Gospel-Centered Life, The Holy Spirit, Grow in Grace, Let's Study Philippians*, and *Some Pastors and Teachers*. His writing interests have ranged from scholarly works to books for children.

He has served as minister of two congregations in Scotland, one on Unst, the most northerly inhabited island in the United Kingdom, and the other in the center of Glasgow, the largest city in Scotland.